WRITER'S GUIDE

Political Science

ARTHUR W. BIDDLE
University of Vermont

KENNETH M. HOLLAND
University of Vermont

with TOBY FULWILER
University of Vermont

D. C. HEATH AND COMPANY
Lexington, Massachusetts   Toronto

Text acknowledgments

"From Bad to Worth" by Charles Krauthammer. Reprinted by permission of *The New Republic*, © 1984, The New Republic, Inc.

From the *Social Sciences Citation Index®*. Reprinted with permission from the *Social Sciences Citation Index®* 1984 Annual. Copyright 1985 by the Institute for Scientific Information®, Philadelphia, PA, USA.

From *International Political Science Abstracts*, pp. 89 and 568 of Volume 34, No. 1–2. Reprinted by permission.

From the *Index to Legal Periodicals*, © 1984, 1985 by the H. W. Wilson Company, p. 527. Materials reproduced by permission of the publisher.

Preface

The best way to learn political science is by writing it — that's the principle behind this book. *Writer's Guide: Political Science* applies current writing theory to the special needs of this exciting discipline. The result is a powerful aid for students of political science at every level.

TO THE STUDENT

Whether you are a committed political science major or an engineer taking an elective, whether you are enrolled in your first political science course or your last, if you want to understand this challenging field, *Writer's Guide* is meant for you. This book shows you how to keep abreast of current events, explains why policy analysis has become so prevalent (and teaches you how to write one), even demystifies the legal brief. You'll find help with all your political science writing needs.

TO THE INSTRUCTOR

Written by a political scientist and a writing specialist, *Writer's Guide: Political Science* offers a variety of resources adaptable to virtually any course in your curriculum. Introductory students might find the first three or four chapters most valuable, leading up to a one-paragraph research essay, a clipping file, or, more ambitiously, an issue analysis and argument. Those chapters would also prove useful for intermediate level students, but their major piece of writing might be policy analysis or a research proposal, as explained in Chapters 5 and 6. Advanced students could write a research proposal and then conduct the research and write up their findings. Or, they might prepare a policy analysis. Every student required to do library work will find the chapter on library research and materials goes beyond a mere introduction to the building.

Keeping a journal (as explained in Chapter 2) seems to bring out the best in just about every student from freshman to graduate. Finally, concise guides to usage and punctuation provide handy reference aids.

Each chapter of *Writer's Guide* is designed to be self-instructional. Although the value of many assignments would be enhanced by class discussion, students can use this book independently. The purpose of several chapters is to guide the reader/writer through the steps of researching and writing a major paper. In the chapter on issue analysis, for instance, the reader learns how to select an issue, then how to analyze that issue, and finally how to take a stand. Each step culminates in a writing assignment, each assignment leads to the next, until the student has produced a finished essay. Undoubtedly, some instructors will simply assign a chapter as a means of assigning a paper. However you choose to use this book, we believe that it will improve your students' understanding of political science, not just their writing ability.

Acknowledgements

The authors joyfully express their appreciation to many people for their assistance in the preparation of this book. Our greatest debt is owed to our students. In writing classes as well as political science courses, students field-tested most of this material and gave very practical advice for improvements. The majority of writing samples in this book came out of those classes. We're grateful to the authors for permission to use their work.

We also had a lot of help from friends and colleagues. At the University of Vermont Lynne Bond, Virginia Clark, Mary Jane Dickerson, Toby Fulwiler, William Haltom, Littleton Long, Anthony Magistrale, and Henry Steffens have been especially supportive. From neighboring Saint Michael's College Daniel Bean and Jennie Versteeg read chapters in progress and made suggestions. Political scientists and writing specialists at other colleges and universities helped too: Mary Thornberry, Davidson College; William Lasser, Clemson University; and Philip Chapman, University of Arizona.

Arthur W. Biddle
Kenneth M. Holland
Burlington, Vermont

Contents

[1] *Writing in Political Science*

PREVIEW: *Writing is a powerful way of learning.
This chapter explains the value of writing in political
science courses and illustrates the decisions you need
to make before starting out.*
   Why write?
   You and the writing process
     Prewriting
     Drafting
     Revising
   The writer's decisions
     Subject
     Purpose
     Audience
     Voice

WHY WRITE?

That's a pretty good question. You enrolled in a political science course, not a writing workshop, but now you find that you're expected to produce a lot of writing. Why? Here are some good reasons:

Writing will help you learn political science. You've probably discovered the principle behind this fact already: We learn best, not as passive recipients of lectures and textbooks, but as active participants, making meaning for ourselves. Writing is one of the best ways to get involved in your own education. That's what this book is all about — writing to learn. Your personal involvement through writing will lead you to a fuller understanding of political science.

Writing clarifies your understanding of the subject. Let's say you read a chapter in your textbook or listen to a fifty-minute lecture on the federal deficit and understand most of it. Writing what you comprehend helps you review, organize, and remember the material. But some of the information still puzzles you. By putting your questions on paper, by writing about your confusion, you begin to see just where the difficulty lies. Often, you can write your way to understanding. Even if that doesn't work, you'll know which sections of the chapter to reread or which notes to review. You can ask your professor an intelligent question: for instance, which special interest groups might favor reducing the deficit?

Writing reveals your attitude toward a subject. An assignment might be to read two articles about U.S. foreign policy in Central America. As you study one of the essays, you agree with that writer's position. Then you read another piece and are persuaded to that point of view. Does that sound familiar? Professional writers can be persuasive — that's their line of work. That we readers sometimes have trouble assessing what we read shouldn't surprise us. What to do? Listing the pros and cons of a given policy helps you see the strengths and weaknesses of each side. Writing can help you discover how you feel about the issue. Then you're on the way to defining your own position.

Writing helps you synthesize large amounts of information. The human mind is a marvel unduplicated by the most advanced computer. Still, most of us don't seem to command the kind of memory we need. Making notes supplements memory and provides access to limitless information. That's why note taking is an essential part of research. Further, you can understand how the information you have collected is related by writing about it. Writing allows you to discover new ways of solving a problem.

Writing organizes your thoughts. You already know that. When you have a lot to accomplish, you make a list of "things to do today." When you prepare a speech or a class presentation, you jot down main ideas, then reorganize them into some sort of meaningful pattern. Combining invisible thoughts with the physical activity of forming words on paper helps you to see what you're thinking. Somehow the need to commit your thinking to the page focuses the energy of your mind. That sounds sort of mystical, but that's what seems to happen.

Learning through writing may seem to take longer, but you'll find that it leads to a fuller understanding of the subject. And you'll like your new-found control of your studies. You've taken charge!

YOU AND THE WRITING PROCESS

Has this ever happened to you? Your professor assigns a paper, due at the end of the semester. You're not told much more about it — perhaps you get a list of acceptable topics or learn how many pages to write. Then, despite your best intentions, you wait until a couple of days before the due date to get started. This is an old and sad story.

There are better ways of doing things. Whether you need to write a term paper, a seminar presentation, or a book review — virtually any communication, in fact — the most effective means is **the process approach.** Using this method of composition, you work your way through three broad stages: **prewriting, drafting,** and **revising.** Most experienced writers work this way. Writers-in-training seem to make the greatest improvement when they practice composing in this fashion.

Prewriting

All the preparations the writer makes before starting to draft — that's what we mean by prewriting. Among these preparations are finding a topic, limiting that topic to manageable size, defining purpose, assessing audience, choosing a point of view, researching or interviewing, and taking notes. This prewriting stage of the process is much more crucial than many realize. When you know that, you're ahead of the rest. And when you master these preparations, you win a new control over your writing. You'll take the first steps in the next section, The Writer's Decisions, and in Chapter 2, Keeping a Journal. You will also find help with prewriting throughout this book, as you learn how to jot down plans and outlines and to write a discovery draft.

Drafting

The second stage of the composing process, drafting, is what most people have in mind when they think of writing. Drafting is getting the words down on paper, much easier when you use the process approach. Later chapters will guide you through this stage.

Revising

Revising, the third stage, involves much more than most writers-in-training suspect. Example: This chapter is now in its sixth draft. In other words, it has been revised five times. That's why professional writers have such big wastebaskets — they keep working on a piece until it's right. Look up the word *revise* in the dictionary; you will find that it comes from the Latin *revidere* — to see again. True revision means just that, seeing again, looking once more at a draft with a willingness to consider changes, often big changes. You'll learn more about making these changes as you proceed through this book. Then, after you've revised your way to a good piece of work, refer to Chapter 9, A Concise Guide to Usage, and Chapter 10, Make Punctuation Work for You, for help with editing. Editing and proofreading are the final steps before submitting your work to reader or editor.

THE WRITER'S DECISIONS

During the prewriting phase, before beginning to draft, the writer confronts several questions: Why am I writing this? Who's going to read it? What will they be expecting? How should my voice sound? Consciously or not, writers must answer these questions each time they sit down to write. Whether you are researching a term paper for your American government course, or applying to law school, or writing a textbook for a course in international relations, the questions are the same. Only the answers are different.

What is this piece about?
Your answer to this question establishes the **subject,** the true topic of this piece of writing.

Why am I writing this? What do I want this to do?
In answering these questions you make decisions about purpose. **Purpose** is your intent, the reason that moves you to write, and the desired result of that effort.

Whom am I writing this for?
The answer to this question identifies your audience. **Audience** is the reader or readers you are addressing.

Who am I as I write this?

The answer to this question defines your voice. **Voice** is the character, personality, and attitudes you project toward your subject, toward your purpose, and toward your audience.

Subject, purpose, audience, and voice are controls in any job of writing. Once you make decisions or accept conditions concerning their natures, you establish certain parameters. Style, tone, readability, even organization and use of examples, are all governed by these initial choices.

The figure below is an attempt to show how the four decisions relate to each other. At the heart of the figure is **subject,** the focus of any piece of writing and usually the writer's first decision. The connecting lines suggest the influence that subject has on purpose, audience, and voice, as well as the relationship they have to one another.

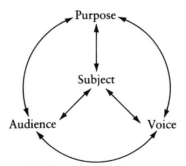

Figure 1.1 *The Writer's Decisions.*

Decision 1: Subject

Finding something to write about is often the hardest of the prewriting tasks for writers-in-training. In the "real world," of course, you would write only when you had something to say, perhaps to yourself in your journal or perhaps when you felt the need to express it to others. In college courses, however, you are often told to write, whether you need to or not. That's because your professors view the writing process as a means of learning. One objective in most political science courses is learning to perceive the world as a political scientist. That means asking the questions and formulating the problems in the same ways that a practicing political scientist does.

One of the best solutions to this problem of finding a **subject** is to anticipate it. Keeping a political science journal will provide you with dozens of ideas for writing. In Chapter 2, Keeping a Journal, you'll learn how it is done.

Whatever subject you choose to write about should meet the following specifications:

1. It should fit the assignment. Does the subject fall into the scope of the course? A paper on limiting the nuclear arms race or imports of Japanese autos, for instance, is inappropriate for a course in constitutional law. Does the paper come within the limits established by the assignment? An account of Franklin D. Roosevelt's attempt to pack the Supreme Court would not fit the assignment, "Write a paper about a *current* issue of public policy."

2. It should be of interest to you. An obvious criterion, but one that students often overlook. If you are to spend thirty or forty hours researching and writing a paper, you should feel some intellectual excitement about the subject. Of course, you might discover a new interest as you read about a topic you thought dull at first. But to the extent possible, begin with a question you genuinely want to answer.

3. It should be limited to allow adequate depth and breadth of coverage. If the assignment calls for a six- to eight-page paper, a topic like "the foreign policy of the United States toward Western Europe" is doomed to failure. Trying to cover two hundred years of relations with a dozen very different nations is hopeless. Limiting that broad topic could yield some very workable subjects, though: economic issues in U.S.–West German relations in the 1970s, for example, or deployment of U.S. missiles in Western Europe.

> WRITING 1.1: FINDING A SUBJECT. Write a list of five topics, suitable for a six- to eight-page paper, from the broad subject: the foreign policy of the United States toward Western Europe.

Decision 2: Purpose

The **purpose** of a piece of writing can be complex, for it includes both the reason that moves you to write and the desired outcome. If you're writing a book review because your professor told you to, the professor's requirement provides one dimension of purpose. That requirement is not sufficient purpose to generate an effective review, however. You need to question yourself more closely: Why am I asked to write this? What does a book review do? You may then decide that you were asked to do the review to get you to read the book, think about it, and summarize the main points of the book and their relationship to the course.

Very likely all the political science writing you will ever do will have as its general purpose either to explain or to persuade. A further classification of kinds of explanation or exposition, as it is often called, will be useful.

- **Definition.** Used to answer the question, "What is it?" of your subject. *Example:* "What is democracy?"
- **Classification.** Used to answer the question, "What is the pattern?" of your subject. *Example:* "What are the various forms of government?"
- **Comparison and Contrast.** Used to answer the question, "What is it like or unlike?" of your subject. *Example:* "What are the similarities and differences between communism and fascism?"
- **Analysis.** Used to answer the question, "What are the relationships among the parts?" of your subject. *Example:* "What are the major features of the U.S. Constitution?"

And, if your purpose combines explanation and persuasion:

- **Argumentation.** Used to answer the question, "Can you prove it?" of your subject. *Example:* "Should the United States support efforts to overthrow unfriendly governments in Central America?"

WRITING 1.2: DEFINING PURPOSE. Begin with the broad subject: the two-party system in the United States. Then ask of that subject the questions listed above: for instance, "What is the two-party system in the United States?" Write your responses. The purpose of this exercise is to learn how

7

these purposes can help you sharpen a subject and focus your writing.

Decision 3: Audience

When you speak, you always speak to someone. That someone is your **audience.** It may be just one person, a group of friends, or your entire class. You know who the listener is and can see and hear reactions; you can tailor your talk to that audience, even modifying it according to the responses you get. When you write, however, your audience is unseen and perhaps even unknown. If it doesn't understand something you write, it cannot ask you to explain yourself. These differences between the speaker-listener relationship and the writer-reader relationship point out the importance of the writer's decisions about audience.

Just as you need to define the purpose of a piece of writing, you also need to define the audience. Let's take an example: The chairman of the political science department asks you to write a short essay to be titled, "Why Major in Political Science?" If you agree to do the job, what additional information will you need? Certainly you need to know who is going to read this — what is your audience? The professor tells you that your essay will appear in a brochure to be distributed to students. Ah, but which students? Entering freshmen undecided about a major? High school seniors shopping around for a college? Upperclassmen considering a change of major? Although the **subject** seems to remain the same (reasons to major in political science), the requirements of these three audiences are somewhat different. You can write much more persuasively if you can define your audience precisely.

What exactly does the writer need to know about the audience for a particular piece of writing? Although the answers to that question depend partly on the **purpose** of the writing, here are some useful questions to ask:

What is the gender of the audience? the age? job? income?

What is the audience's educational level? religion?

What does the audience already know about the subject?

What are its expectations likely to be? its attitudes?

What other special needs of this audience should you take into account?

Only by raising these questions will you discover which ones you need to concern yourself with as you plan a piece. By asking these questions about the audience of "Why Major in Political Science?" you get a much better idea of how to slant that writing.

What about defining the audience of writing you do in this course? Because student writers often have a great deal of trouble with that decision, you should know the options.

1. You can write for the professor, the most common way of defining the audience of a student paper. The problem with addressing this audience lies in your defining exactly who your professor is and what his or her expectations are.
2. You can write for the entire class, students and professor. If you do, you are likely to be less pompous and more direct than you would be addressing the professor alone. Why is that? How else might your work differ?
3. You can write for yourself, as you might in a journal (see Chapter 2). Practically every writer-in-training would benefit from producing more of this writer-based prose.
4. You can write for a specified audience, such as registered voters, people opposed to a constitutional amendment calling for a balanced budget, or your congressional representative.
5. You can write for scholars in the field, as if you were composing an article for a professional journal. The best way to get a sense of this audience's expectations is to read several articles in political science journals. See Chapter 7, Principles of Research, for suggestions.

WRITING 1.3: DEFINING AUDIENCE. Choose a topic that you are currently studying, like states' rights under the federal system or amending the Constitution. Write an explanation of the ways that you might adapt your treatment of that topic for each of the five audiences listed above. Be specific about audience expectations and needs and about adjustments you might make.

Decision 4: Voice

"Who am I as I write this review or essay or whatever?" Although the question may seem silly, it really isn't. Your **voice** is the character, personality, and attitudes you project toward your subject, toward your purpose, and toward your audience. It is the "you" that you have deliberately chosen to express **on this occasion.**

Your writing voice, like your speaking voice, should be appropriate for the situation in which you find yourself or which you define. You don't use the same voice with your parents that you use with your best friend. You don't use the same voice with your professor that you use with your roommate. Because we have so much experience talking with others, we adopt the appropriate speaking voice almost without thinking about it.

When we begin to write, however, we need to confront the choices consciously and to weigh a number of complex factors. Consider this variety of possible attitudes affecting your voice:

Subject: treat it seriously, lightly, humorously, reverently?

Purpose: praise, abuse, ask a favor, explain a process, encourage, persuade, complain?

Audience: peers, enemies, professor, lover, fellow vegetarians, other conservatives or liberals?

Occasion: formal, informal, ceremonious?

Clearly, these options are interdependent: that is, a writer probably wouldn't ask a favor in an abusive voice or complain to someone in authority in a humorous one. Your task as a writer is to match the voice to the occasion, the subject, the purpose, and the audience.

Just how do you convey a voice, once you've selected one? **Word choice** is one means. To the sensitive writer most so-called synonyms aren't equal. *Abdicate, resign, quit,* and *walk out* might mean roughly the same, but they aren't identical in meaning or in voice. Some words are simple and straightforward, others seem more formal. The distinction is made obvious in this pair of sentences that have the same meaning but different voices:

"She purveys Mollusca at the pelagic area."
"She sells seashells at the sea shore."

Another stylistic element that conveys voice is **sentence structure.** A long, complex sentence might be more appropriate for a relatively formal treatment of a serious subject for educated readers, whereas a series of short, declarative sentences could be more apt for informal treatment of the same subject for the same audience.

Even **punctuation** helps establish voice. A semicolon, for example, is a fairly formal mark of punctuation. Writing in an informal voice, you would probably avoid that mark in favor of separating the clauses with a period. Dashes and exclamation marks generally have an informal effect. See Chapter 10 for other punctuation guidelines.

Voice, audience, purpose, and subject — these are the key prewriting decisions. Making knowledgeable choices about each — that is your job as writer.

WRITING 1.4: DEFINING VOICE.   Explain what voice you think would be appropriate for each of your responses in Writing 1.3. Be specific and explain how concerns of subject and purpose influence your decisions.

[2] *Keeping a Journal*

TOBY FULWILER

PREVIEW: *Writing in a journal will help you*
understand political science and the world around you.
In this chapter you will learn what a journal is and
how to use one.
 Why keep a journal?
 What is a journal?
 Characteristics of journals
 Suggestions for your journal
 What to write

Keeping a journal can help you learn political science. The journal
is the place to record observations, speculate, raise questions, and
figure things out. Journals have been used for such purposes for a
long time, but only recently have they become widely used in college. Most serious thinkers, writers, scientists, artists, philosophers,
prime ministers, and generals have kept something like a journal in
which to capture their thoughts. St. Augustine and Jean-Jacques
Rousseau based their "confessions" on their journals. Most of our
Founding Fathers kept journals, as did authors like Anne Brad-
street, Ralph Waldo Emerson, and Henry David Thoreau. The in-
fluential modern thinkers of our century — Darwin, Marx, Freud,
and Einstein — recorded their questions and tentative answers in
journals.

Samuel Pepys, seventeenth-century essayist, called his journal a
"diary." Edward Weston, the photographer, called his a "daybook."
Albert Camus, the French novelist, called his simply a "notebook."
Still others have called them "logs" or "commonplace books." Of
course, it doesn't matter what this record of daily thought is called.
What matters is that you understand why it can be useful and how
it works.

If you have never kept a journal before, you might have some
questions: What, exactly, is a journal? What does one look like?

Why should I keep a journal? Aren't they something for poets rather than serious social scientists? If I do keep one, what and when should I write in it? Above all, what can it do for me in this class? How can it possibly help me learn more about political science? Let's look at some answers.

WHY KEEP A JOURNAL?

The act of writing helps people understand things better. Formal research as well as our own experience as students and teachers demonstrate this truth. If you are a student of political science and you write about ideas, issues, and problems you are studying, you will begin to sort out those ideas, issues, and problems more clearly. Any assignment can be made richer by reflecting about it in your journal: What do I care about? What do I want to know? What have I forgotten that I might remember if I wrote about it?

Writing helps you sort out and retrieve all sorts of information, ideas, and impressions already existing somewhere in your head. Notice what happens when you write letters to friends — how often you begin writing with one thing on your mind and then surprise yourself by bringing up all kinds of other matters. The same thing often happens when you write from an outline — you actually start digressing and going somewhere you never intended. And you like where you have gone and so need to adjust the outline accordingly. That's one of the remarkable powers of the writing process: It doesn't just reflect or communicate your thinking, it actually *leads* it! In other words, writing is a powerful mode of thinking.

Sometimes writing tells you flatly that you can't go where you thought you could. "Hmm, I thought I could explain that better than this. Maybe it's not such a hot idea." As you try to explain to yourself, you see the holes and recognize that you need more information. Learning when you are about to step onto thin ice can be a real survival skill — better to find that out in a private journal than in a public examination. Then you have time to do something about it: read more, research more, ask more questions, or whatever. Writing in your journal about what you don't know is one of the best ways to start knowing.

Your journal will be a place for thinking. Use it to monitor class progress, to write daily plans, to rehearse for class discussions, to

14

practice for examinations, and as a seedbed from which to generate research and term papers. Learn to trust that it will do that. Notebooks can be turned into journals when writers speculate on the meaning of someone else's information and ideas. Personal reflections about political history can help you identify with and perhaps make sense of the otherwise distant and confusing past. Trial hypotheses about political behavior might find first articulation in this same journal. Continued writing about theoretical ideas can develop those ideas into full-fledged research designs.

WHAT IS A JOURNAL?

I can give you an easy explanation first: Journals assigned in class are part diary and part course notebook. But a journal is also distinctly different from each. Diaries record the private thought and experience of the writer. Class notebooks record the public thought and presentation of the teacher. The journal is somewhere between the two. Like the diary, the journal is written in the first person ("I") about ideas important to the writer; like the class notebook, the journal may focus on academic subjects the writer needs to learn more about. We could represent the journal this way:

$$\text{Diary} \rightarrow \text{Journal} \leftarrow \text{Class Notebook}$$
$$(\text{``I''}) \qquad (\text{``I/it''}) \qquad (\text{``it''})$$

Journals may be focused narrowly on the subject matter of political science or broadly on the whole range of your academic and personal experience. Each journal entry is a deliberate exercise in expansion: "How far can I take this idea? How accurately can I describe or explain it? How can I make it make sense to me?" The journal encourages you to become conscious, through language, of what is happening around you, both personally and academically.

CHARACTERISTICS OF JOURNALS

What's unique about journals is that they convey thought trapped in time — like moths trapped in amber. They offer an organizational pattern quite different from that of more traditional assignments. "Chronology" rather than "theme" provides the unity and sets these pieces apart from other academic compositions. But while single journal entries are locked together in time, the collection as a whole may, in fact, transcend time to reveal more complex, often lucid, patterns of growth, development, and understanding. Unlike formal papers, journals carry with them all the time-bound fragments of thought since discarded, modified, or forgotten. Readers of journals, whether the writer or a teacher, get lots of chaff along with the wheat — and find nourishment there as well.

Language, too, sets journals apart. Some of the characteristics of good journal writing may run directly counter to traditional notions about appropriate academic writing. Journals may be full of sentence fragments, digressions, dashes instead of semicolons, frequent references to oneself ("I"), misspellings, shorthand, doodles, sloppy handwriting, self-doubt, and all sorts of unexplained private references and notations. Both distracting and enlightening, these features occur in journals for different reasons than they occur in more formal writing. Journal writers must feel free to use their most comfortable, fast, close-at-hand style at all times. As a result, good journal writing is usually more fun to read — more like personal letters — than more carefully crafted academic prose. The more we trust the value of our own informal voice, the more we will use it both to generate and to communicate ideas.

Consider a journal as a place in which to experiment and play with language, to write often and regularly on a wide variety of topics, to take some risks with form, style, and voice. Notice how writing in the early morning differs from writing late at night. Experience how writing at the same time every day, regardless of inclination or mood, often produces surprising results. Above all else, use your journal as a place to find your easy, natural voice and become comfortable writing it.

SUGGESTIONS FOR YOUR JOURNAL

The following list provides ideas for starting and keeping academic journals in virtually any subject area in college. But remember, these are just suggestions, not commandments. In truth, journals can look like and be anything you and your instructor wish.

1. Buy a small (7" × 10") looseleaf notebook.

2. Divide it into two sections: academic and personal (teacher will collect only the academic section periodically).
3. Date each entry; include time of day.
4. Write in your most comfortable, informal style.
5. Write daily if possible.
6. Write long entries, a new full page each time.
7. Write a personal reaction to every reading and class.
8. Freewrite (fast, without stopping) when you think you have nothing to say.
9. Collect quotes, clippings, scraps of interest.
10. At the end of the term, add table of contents and introduction.

WHAT TO WRITE

You can use a journal as a record of weight loss or as a diary of your personal life. But journals are especially useful for encouraging the very modes of thought most valued in the academic community. The following suggestions may give you some ideas for things to try out in your journal.

1. Observation. Use the journal to record, in your own language, what you see. The simplest observations are sensory experiences, primarily visual, but also aural, tactile, and the like. In more complex observations, try to capture whole experiences or events. In any case, the key to good observation is being there, finding words to capture what you witness, and being able to experience it again when you see it recorded. In political science, observation is a crucial means of collecting data; journals can help you both collect and think about what you collect. Look for details, examples, measurements, facts, analogies, and descriptive language, including color, texture, size, shape, and movement.

2. Speculation. Use your journal to wonder, "What if?" Speculation, in fact, is the essence of good journals, perhaps the very reason for their existence and importance. Journals allow writers to speculate freely, without fear of penalty. Bad speculation and good. Silly as well as productive. Because the bad often clears way for the good and the silly sometimes suggests the serious. Use your journal to think hard about possibilities. No penalties here for free

17

thinking. Look at the first paragraph of a page-long entry written by a student answering the question: "Is the family politically important?"

> 3/11 I think so, yes. Very much so because w/o the
>   family where is civil society? I know that it
>   can't possibly simply be the result of the
>   family. After all, there is a social contract,
>   isn't there? I don't think I've signed it, but
>   I have authorized, indirectly, that someone
>   else sign it for me. I have done this by not
>   objecting to or rebelling against society.

This student is thinking out loud on paper. He starts to make one answer and soon finds himself speculating on whether or not he signed "a social contract." It doesn't matter that he did or didn't sign the contract. (Did you? How do you know? Write about it!) What matters is that the writing provoked the thinking — and the thinking is about an issue central to the study of political science. By relating the issue to his or her own life, the student stands a much greater chance of understanding the issue of "social contract."

3. Questions. Express your curiosity in writing; good thinkers ask lots of questions, perhaps more than they are able to answer. Questions indicate that something is happening — in this case, that there may be some disequilibrium or uncertainty in your mind, and that you are willing to explore it through language. Again, the ability to see one's questions certainly helps one sharpen, clarify, and understand them better. Sometimes writers use journals to record their doubts and uncertainties — one of the few places in the academic world where such frank admissions of ignorance have a place. (It may be all right to admit orally, after class, that you don't know an answer or understand something; it is something else altogether to admit it on an examination or formal essay.) In the journal, one expects to write about what one does not know as well as what one does know. Another name for a journal? A doubt book. Don't be afraid to write, "What's that supposed to mean?" and "I just don't get this." In fact, in journals, it's as important to ask such questions as to answer them. Look at these questions jotted by a political science major in his journal:

```
10/5   Politics is power? Poly sci is the study of
       power? Who gets what where and when. What is
       power? Poly sci is interdisciplinary? Poly
       sci is the study of individual interests?
       Poly sci is the study of organizations!!
```

The writer seems to be playing here with questions. In fact, I suspect he's even playing with the answers he poses. But the playing is, I think, purposeful — even necessary — to gaining a mastery and an understanding of one's subject. Another student writing in answer to the question: Is everything that is good also pleasant? writes: "Yes. No. I don't know. What is good anyway?" Nice.

4. Awareness. Learn who you are, record where you are, think about where you want to go. Be conscious of yourself as a learner, thinker, or writer. Self-awareness is necessary to both higher-order reasoning and mature social interactions. Journals are places where writers can actually monitor and witness the evolution of this process. You can encourage yourself to become more aware by asking lots of questions and trying out lots of answers: "What am I learning in here? What do I remember about today's lecture? The assigned reading? What has any of this got to do with reality? With me? Why am I studying poli sci? Getting this degree?" In the following entry, a student reflects on a question posed by his political science professor: Is greed good or bad? Though the writer starts off answering the question abstractly, he soon turns it back to himself and his own values.

```
2/24   Greed is bad in some cases. Greed is good in
       some cases. It is not an absolute notion to
       be sure. For some instances, like gaining
       power or wealth and then distributing it to
       the poor, that is good. However if 100 people
       die in one's effort . . . that is bad.
            I think as far as greed is concerned
       either I can (could) leave it at that or I
       could write a 100-page discourse. However, I
       don't really want to do that; I am not that
```

> greedy. This is interesting. I do not think I
> am all that greedy in general. I am not that
> greedy because power, among other things, is
> not that important to me. I am not a power
> monger. I like fame and fortune (probably in
> actuality, I don't really like fame and for-
> tune — but I am supposed to like it — but
> why?).

In this case, the student's journal entry actually ends up in a contradiction — one that the writer seems acutely aware of: Is he greedy for some things and not others? Does he like "fame and fortune" or not? The value for the writer, if not the teacher, is that the journal is a place in which to become conscious of one's conflicting goals and values. Maybe later, in another entry or letter or conversation, this student will pick up the threads we see dangling here.

5. Connections. Make the study of political science relevant to everything else in your life — or try to. Can you make connections? Force connections? Find easy connections? To other courses or other events in your life? Journals encourage such connecting because no one is insisting that writers stick to one organized, well-documented subject. Connections can be loose or tight, tangential or direct; the point is, they are connections made by the writer (you), not somebody else. Digressions are also connections; they indicate that something is happening to trigger your memory, to bring forth information and ideas stored in your long-term memory. In journals, value them. Here is a sample journal entry written by a student attending college in Michigan's upper peninsula; the connections are obvious:

> 10/10 I don't know if I'm just over-reacting to my
> Conservation class or not, but lately I've
> become suspicious of the air, water, and
> food around me. First we're taught about
> water pollution, and I find out that the
> Portage Canal merrily flowing right in front
> of my house is unfit for human contact be-
> cause of the sewage treatment plant and how
> it overflows with every hard rain. Worse
> yet, I'm told raw sewage flows next to

```
Bridge Street. I used to admire Douglass
Houghton Falls for its natural beauty, now
all I think of is, "That's raw untreated
sewage flowing there."
     Our next topic was air pollution. Today
I was informed that the rain here in the
U.P. has acid levels ten times what it
should, thanks to sulfur oxide pollution
originating in Minneapolis and Duluth. . . .
     Is there any escaping this all—encom-
passing wave of pollution? I had thought the
Copper Country was a refuge from the poison-
ous fact of pollution, but I guess it's not
just Detroit's problem anymore.
     As I write these words, in countless
places around the globe, old Mother Nature
is being raped in the foulest way. I get the
feeling that someday she'll retaliate and
we'll deserve it. Every bit of it.
```

Here it really doesn't matter in which class or at what time this writing occurred. The value is in having some place to record how one's school learning relates to the rest of one's life — in this case, to the writer's own back yard.

6. Dialogue. Use your journal to talk to your teacher. Have a conversation, find out some things about each other — things perhaps too tangential or personal for class, but which build relationships all the same. When journals are assigned by instructors in academic settings, there is an explicit contract between student and teacher that entries related to thinking about political science will be shared. Consider this journal as "dialogical." Do not expect absolute, complete candor of each other — that's unrealistic. But journals can help you learn more about each other as co-learners if you share entries from time to time, either out loud in class or privately through written responses in the journal itself.

7. Information. Collect and comment on everything you can find that relates to political science. Ironically, in a journal such information may be the least interesting material you collect; usually it serves more as record than anything else. A former student called the pages in which he recorded lecture notes "Cliff Notes stuff" and wished it were in his class notebook, not his journal. However, such references — especially when connected with some personal reaction — supply writers with valuable insights about otherwise rather distant material. Comment on formulae, ideas, outlines, summaries from books, lectures, or class discussions. Here is a brief example of a student's thinking about Edmund Burke:

```
1/26   From what Burke says on the surface we are
       led to believe that the principle of equality
       is for him significant. I believe, however,
       that there exists a discrepancy between what
       he states and what he truly believes . . . he
       does not openly profess that people of dif-
       ferent social class and upbringing are in-
       nately unequal. He tries to conceal this by
       saying those people of lower rank could also
       aspire to political office, though I believe
       he clearly denies this possibility.
```

The entry marks the student's thinking about one specific point in her reading. Because she stops to make this reflection, she almost guarantees that she will remember it.

8. Revision. Consider your journal as a repository for scraps of thought for later development or revision. Journals are also places in which to rethink previous ideas. Try looking back in your journal to see if you can find places where you have since changed your mind on a subject. Then write about what you now think and why you changed your mind. Anne Berthoff, a professor at the University of Massachusetts, advocates what she calls a "double-entry journal," in which writers return periodically to reflect upon previous entries. In other words, build opportunities for revision into the journal itself. At other times, consider the journal as a place in which to start formal papers — to make several starts — until one idea begins to develop a life of its own. Then go with that one — as far as you can until it busts loose from your journal altogether. A good source for first drafts.

9. Problem Posing and Solving. Use your journal to pose as well as solve problems. Don't make the posing something only teachers and experts do; use your journal to help here. Whether the problem is posed well, or whether the solution actually works, matters little. (If the problems are consistently ill-defined and the solutions always off base, that does matter. Here, though, the journal will be invaluable in another way, as an early clue to where you are really having trouble.) According to Brazilian educator Paulo Friere, individuals must articulate problems in their own language in order to experience authentic growth. Journals are, perhaps, the best place in the academic world in which to do that. Evidence of posing and solving problems — whether literary, social, scientific, or mechanical — suggests that you're alive, thoughtful, and perhaps even committed. Look at the problem articulated by a student of political philosophy:

```
2/18   Political philosophy is often interesting.
       However, I have discovered a specific problem
       that I'm not sure how to solve. For that mat-
       ter, I'm not sure if (1) it can be solved or
       (2) it should be solved. . . . Each time we
       read a new political philosopher we learn
       that what he says is somehow better, more ad-
       vanced, or more accurate than what the last
       guy said. This is troubling me because each
       time we read a new author -- and it started
       with Machiavelli or Hobbes -- we (I) take
       this to be the "end all." It is right and
       nothing else is. But this cannot be.
          Everything each new philosopher says
       cannot be right and better than the last. Why
       is this so? . . . that because the previous
       guy wrote what he did the subsequent guy
       wrote what he did. If the first guy hadn't
       written, probably the second wouldn't have
       been spurred on to write what he did.
```

The point, of course, is not so much that the writer finds a sophisticated or authoritative answer — he doesn't — but that he works out an answer to a problem that has suddenly confronted him. This entry, like some of the other samples we have looked at, illustrates several modes of thought taking place in rapid succession: asking questions, expressing doubt, analyzing a problem, and trying out a solution. It also illustrates the kind of journal entry which summarizes, at least temporarily, a student's overall reaction to his whole course of study. In that sense, it is also an example of the last suggestion I will make here: synthesis.

10. Synthesis. One of the best and most practical activities for your journal is to synthesize, daily and weekly, what's going on in your study of political science: "How does this lecture relate to the last one? What do I expect next time? How does class discussion relate to the stated objectives on the syllabus?" Your written answers to any of these questions can easily generate comments to share with both class and teacher. If you can take even five minutes at the end of each class — or stay in your seat five minutes after class — you can catch perceptions and connections that will otherwise escape you as you run off to another class, lunch, or a quick snooze back at your room. Journals invite you to put together what you learn. If you let journal writing work for you in some of the ways suggested in this chapter, I think you'll gradually learn to be both a better learner and a better writer. Journals aren't magic. But the practice of daily speculative writing will exercise your mind in much the same way that running or swimming exercises your body. The practice of writing to oneself can become a useful regular habit: Try fifteen minutes each morning with coffee, twenty minutes each evening before homework, or even ten minutes before bed. You will find writing in it easier and easier and, in time, may find it a mentally restful activity — the one time in a busy schedule to put your life in order. And at the end of the term or after you graduate, you'll find this marvelous written record of your thoughts, beliefs, problems, solutions, and dreams. The nice thing about the journal is that it represents a powerful process while you keep it and, at the same time, it results in a wonderfully personal product.

[3] *Learning Political Science Through Writing*

PREVIEW: *An understanding of political science depends on the mastery of a number of reading and writing skills. This chapter explains some of the relationships between reading and writing and teaches you how to write an abstract, a book review, a legal brief, and other forms.*

> *Reading for main ideas, writing to summarize (I)*
> > *Summary*
> > *Abstract*
> > *Book Review*
> *Learning to synthesize*
> *Understanding contemporary affairs*
> *Expressing an opinion*
> > *Letters to the editor*
> > *Letters to public officials*
> *Reading for main ideas, writing to summarize (II)*
> > *Briefing court decisions*

Politics is no exact science.

—Otto von Bismarck

Earlier in this book we claimed that writing is an invaluable way to learn political science. Writing helps you discover what you know and what you think. Writing leads your thinking toward new insights.

If you've been keeping a journal, following the suggestions in the last chapter, you probably are beginning to agree — writing does help you to ask questions, make connections, pose and solve problems, even synthesize and create new knowledge. Your journal is a great personal tool for thinking about the world as a political place. But what happens when you need to go public? How do you meet those demands made by professor or boss to write to a larger audience than yourself?

You'll find some of the answers here in this chapter, where the focus is on writing short analytical assignments. Reading for main ideas, writing to summarize, learning to synthesize, understanding contemporary affairs, taking a stand — each of these topics bears on an important intellectual activity and a related type of writing. They're not simple answers. Writing isn't easy. But if you work at it, you'll develop abilities that will take you through your college years and beyond — through graduate school or law school, into your first job, and throughout your life.

READING FOR MAIN IDEAS, WRITING TO SUMMARIZE (I)

The connection between reading and writing is nowhere more evident than in the production of an abstract or summary. Whether you think of yourself as a reader writing or as a writer reading, first you must discover the thrust and main ideas of a journal article or book and then convey that information precisely.

Reading for Main Ideas

Reading for main ideas is not all that different from the kind of reading you do when you study new material in a textbook. The purpose is to identify and extract the gold from all that ore, in other words to find the thesis, or assertion, of the article or book chapter and the supporting points. But how do you locate those main ideas? To a large extent, the material you work with will determine the approach you take: Each article or book will differ in organization and presentation. But because most professional writers follow certain rules of organization, we can offer some basic principles of reading here that are generally applicable. Applying these hints should help you understand most material.

Perhaps the simplest, yet one of the most effective reading strategies, is to use the typographical signals in the text itself. Just as route numbering signs are intended to lead the driver through an unfamiliar city, typographical signals are meant as signposts to guide the reader through the maze of the text. Begin by thinking about the title of the article or book. Don't overlook the subtitle, if there is one. These features identify the subject and often the scope of the work. Chapter and section headings tell you what is to come. Within paragraphs look for words printed in **bold face** and *italic* type, indicating important terms or concepts. Supporting data is usually summarized in a graph or figure; if the significance of that data is not clear, look to the corresponding section of text.

Another reading strategy is to look for key ideas in the obvious places. If you are dealing with an entire book, look to find the thesis, scope, and method explained in the preface or introduction. For an article or book chapter, look for the thesis at the end of the first paragraph or the beginning of the second paragraph. Within the piece, main ideas are ordinarily where you would expect to find them — at the beginning (or, less commonly, at the end) of each paragraph.

Writing to Summarize

Imagine yourself in this situation: You have just spent two hours struggling through a complex article about the relationship of education to voting preferences. As you read, you made notes in order to help yourself decipher the article and remember what it is about. When you arrive in class, your roommate, who barely made it through the first page of the article, pleads, "Quick, fill me in!" And you try. Then your professor enters the classroom and asks you to jot down the key issues in the article. Finally, as you leave the class, you are given the assignment of writing an abstract of the article for your next class meeting.

In each of these four instances you have a need to summarize the material from a journal article. However, the purpose and thus the form and content of each summary is a bit different. In this section we'll explain briefly how to write article summaries as well as a related form, the abstract, and how this process is shaped by your purposes. Let's begin by distinguishing between abstracts and summaries. In general terms, an abstract is a kind of summary, but the term *abstract* has taken on a special meaning in scholarly writing. The abstract in political science (and in the other social sciences as well) has requirements of content and form that have been standardized virtually worldwide. An abstract is formal and impersonal; its format and length are prescribed by the conventions of the discipline. On the other hand, a general summary of a paper or book may be formal or informal, objective or personalized; its form, content, and length may vary to suit the writer's needs. We'll look first at the summary, then at the abstract.

Summary

Just about the only rule that applies to writing a summary is this: Present the basic ideas of the original writing without distortion. The summary's form and content are dictated by its intended purpose, subject, and audience. In the hypothetical example described earlier, you have several reasons for summarizing an article. You might write a summary in your journal to help clarify your thinking about the article. In this case, your summary might or might not be comprehensive and detailed. It might or might not be in a form that would be understood by another reader. This summary might meander back and forth between your personal experience and only one of the themes of the article. Or it might compare this and another article's perspective on a relatively small but significant issue. Alternatively, you might have summarized the article so that you could use it in a research paper you are working on, in which case you'd probably want to be more comprehensive and include all the key points made in the article.

The summary of the article you made for your roommate is likely to be very different. Your purpose here is to communicate a general overview of the information to someone who is unfamiliar with the material. This summary needs to teach another person new information rather than remind you of connections you have already considered. While less comprehensive than your written summary for exam preparation, it must be relatively detailed.

Your five-minute class exercise in jotting down the article's key issues for the professor is unique in yet other ways. Your purpose is to evaluate, that is prioritize, the significance of the issues raised. You must be comprehensive in terms of pointing out key issues, but you need not be particularly detailed on any. You assume that your audience (the professor) is well versed in the area, so your intent is to identify and integrate issues rather than to reiterate details or teach the information to a naive reader.

Because summaries can serve so many differing functions, you should first identify your purposes. The most efficient and effective summary writing is highly sensitive to its intended purpose, audience, and subject matter.

Abstract

The purpose of an abstract is to provide a concise but comprehensive summary of an article or book, a summary that will allow readers to decide whether the article treats information that is of interest to them. Abstracts are ordinarily used in two contexts. The abstract is the first section of any article appearing in a professional or scholarly journal. Abstracts are also used in indexing or information services (e.g. *Social Science Abstracts*) where they are organized by subject, date, etc., to allow readers to systematically search for information of interest. The *Publication Manual of the American Psychological Association* points out, "A well-prepared abstract can be the single most important paragraph in the article. An abstract (a) is read first, (b) may be the only part of an article that is actually read (readers frequently decide, on the basis of the abstract, whether to read the entire article), and (c) is an important means of access in locating and retrieving the article" (American Psychological Association, 1983, p. 23). (Because the APA Manual, as it is familiarly known, has become a standard reference throughout the social sciences, we base our advice here and elsewhere in this book on its recommendations.)

Do you need to worry about how to write an abstract only when you are ready to present your research for publication? Not at all. In addition to the formal purposes mentioned by the APA, composing an abstract serves an important function for you: It forces you to analyze carefully the true essence of the material you're reading or writing. The significance of this process becomes clearer when you understand the specific form and content requirements of a formal abstract. These requirements vary slightly depending on the nature of the article you have to treat. Therefore, we'll consider each type of article and its abstract in turn.

Empirical Research Report

A common kind of article in political science is the **empirical research report,** a presentation of the methodology and findings of field research. (In Chapter 6, you will learn how to write such a report.) An abstract of an empirical research report should be no longer than 150 words — even if the work took five years to complete and the article is 25 pages. The abstract is typed as a single paragraph. According to APA guidelines (1983), it should include the following elements:

1. a statement of the problem investigated (perhaps the hypothesis tested) ideally in no more than one sentence
2. the subjects of the study, including their relevant characteristics, such as number, age, sex, and geographical distribution
3. the research procedure, including special questionnaires, data-gathering techniques, statistical procedures; be as specific as necessary in order to represent their importance in the study
4. the main results of the study
5. the conclusions and implications of the study.

Can Government Regulate Safety? The Coal Mine Example

MICHAEL S. LEWIS-BECK
University of Iowa

JOHN R. ALFORD
Oakland University

With the 1970 passage of the Occupational Safety and Health Act (OSHA), federal regulation reached the American workplace. Given the newness of the legislation, any firm conclusion on its effectiveness seems premature. However, there is ample evidence on federal safety regulation of a specific workplace: the coal mine. The federal government has been directly involved in coal mining safety for over 35 years, operating under three major pieces of legislation, enacted in 1941, 1952, and 1969. Opposing opinions regarding the effect of this legislation can be grouped into three categories: radical, reactionary, and reformer. A multiple interrupted time-series anal-

ysis indicates that, in fact, the 1941 and 1969 regulations significantly reduced the fatality rate in coal mining. Certain conditions seem related to
the effectiveness of this safety legislation: birth order, provisions, enforcement, target population, and goals. The first two conditions would appear
to work for the success of the OSHA, the latter three conditions to work
against it.

Review or Theoretical Article

A second kind of article written by political scientists is the **review
or theoretical article,** which is either a review of the literature in a
subfield or the presentation of a principle of political science. An
abstract of one of these articles is quite similar to that for an empirical report, but is likely to be a bit shorter — 75 to 150 words.
According to APA guidelines (1983) it should include:

1. a brief statement of the topic (one sentence)
2. an indication of the paper's thesis or assertion as well as its
    scope (i.e., whether it is comprehensive or selective)
3. a mention of the types of sources that the article used (e.g.,
    published literature, field research)
4. the conclusions and implications or applications of this article.

The Just and the
Advantageous in Thucydides:
The Case of the Mytilenaian Debate

CLIFFORD ORWIN

The University of Toronto

As no passage in Thucydides is more important, so none is more dramatic
than the Mytilenaian Debate. Having resolved to punish harshly a rebel
city, the Athenians repent and reconsider. Exhorted by Kleon to maintain
their original decision and by Diodotos to abandon it, the Athenians must
scrutinize the relationship between justice and expediency. Diodotos, who

professes to argue from interest only, narrowly prevails in the debate. There is, however, much more to his speech than meets the eye. For it proves misleading to say that he is arguing merely from interest — and then, on a deeper level, to say that he is arguing from justice. In fact no passage in Thucydides, including the Melian Dialogue, raises starker questions about the status of political justice.

Policy Analysis

The third kind of article is the **policy analysis,** the study of alternative solutions to a basic policy problem (see Chapter 5, Policy Analysis). An abstract of a policy analysis is a single paragraph, 75–150 words long, and should include:

1. a brief statement of the policy problem
2. a list of objectives of the ideal solution; that is, the solution which would best solve the problem at the least cost
3. a list of alternative solutions
4. a statement of the optimal solution, that is, the practical solution that comes closest to the ideal solution.

Arbitration and Mediation as Alternatives to Court
CRAIG A. McEWEN AND RICHARD J. MAIMAN

Abstract

Advocates of mediation and arbitration claim their superiority to adjudication in three areas: reduction of court caseloads and costs; increase in accessibility of justice; and improvement in the quality of justice. Available evidence shows that mediation and arbitration neither lower court costs (though they increase court capacity), nor substantially expand access to justice. By some measures, however, mediation provides fairer outcomes and, in civil cases, higher rates of compliance than does adjudication. Though less effective than often claimed in reducing problems of administering justice, mediation and arbitration — in their distinctive ways — do thus offer modestly effective alternatives to court.

32

As you can see, the abstract must be very brief but also comprehensive. That's where the difficulty lies. How can you put all that information into 75–150 words (one third to two thirds of a typed page)? It definitely is not easy. That's why writing an abstract provides such excellent practice in distilling, communicating, and preserving the essence of an article or project. Writing an abstract, whether based on your own research or someone else's, can crystallize your understanding and appreciation of the basic elements of a piece of scholarly writing.

The American Psychological Association (APA, 1983) description is well worth keeping in mind. A good abstract is

1. accurate. The abstract must accurately reflect the paper. Not only should you avoid actual errors in representing the article, but you should also avoid shifting the emphasis. Put nothing in the abstract that isn't in the original.

2. concise and specific. Each sentence should pack as much information as possible. To be concise, be specific. Consider the following portion of an abstract:

```
(a)   One of the issues on the judicial reform
agenda is whether the procedures presently avail-
able to consumers of court services are adequate to
secure the speedy, inexpensive, and just resolution
of disputes. Some commentators vigorously defend
the adequacy of the adversarial framework inherited
from English law; others contend that the tradi-
tional form of adjudication can no longer meet the
needs of an increasingly complex society. Comple-
menting this normative debate is empirical dis-
agreement on just how adversarial the present sys-
tem is. Judging from the objects selected by
researchers for analysis, most students of the ju-
dicial process assume that the system operates in
an adversarial manner. This article seeks to answer
the empirical question for the purposes of redi-
recting research and informing the public and
professional debate over procedural reforms. The
evidence is that since 1938 there has been a sub-
stantial realignment in court activities and proce-
dures and that the system of civil justice is in
fact largely nonadversarial.
```

Not bad, is it? It seems to tell about the article in a fairly condensed fashion. But this abstract is 158 words (over the allowable limit) and wordy to boot. Can you find ways of reducing this example without losing any of the information? Look for repetition. Find unnecessary words. Where would you make changes if this were your abstract?

Here is the kind of revision you might have made:

```
(b)   The author evaluates changes in the form of
civil adjudication that have occurred since the
adoption of the Federal Rules of Civil Procedure in
1938. The evidence reveals a paradoxical situation
-- the system has become both less and more adver-
sarial. After identifying the causes of these op-
posing trends, the author concludes that the forces
undermining adversariness are more powerful than
those supporting the traditional model. Finally,
the implications of this retreat from customary
procedure are explored.
```

We've reduced the material to only 76 words, less than half the original, and have retained all the information of the lengthier version. In fact, readers would probably find it easier to follow than the first version. You shouldn't expect your first attempt to be as brief and concise. In fact, example (a) would serve as a very acceptable first draft of an abstract. Just start by getting down all the essential information, then revise until you've achieved your goal.

3. self-contained. Your abstract should be able to stand on its own without reference to the original paper. You should define acronyms, abbreviations, and unique terms, and spell out the names of uncommon procedures. Paraphrase rather than quote.

4. nonevaluative. Simply report what's in the paper; the abstract is not the place to add your own thoughts and insights.

5. coherent and readable. Use clear prose and active verbs rather than passive voice ("analysis revealed" rather than "it was revealed by analysis"). Use past tense to refer to procedures used or variables manipulated in the study. Use present tense to refer to results that have continuing application and to conclusions drawn.

Elements of an Abstract

For an empirical report
1. the problem
2. the subjects
3. the procedure
4. the results
5. the conclusions, implications

For a theoretical or review article
1. the topic
2. the thesis and scope
3. the sources used
4. the conclusions, implications

For a policy analysis
1. the policy problem
2. objectives of the ideal solution
3. list of alternative solutions
4. the optimal solution

WRITING 3.1: WRITING THE ABSTRACT. We've discussed the form, content, and characteristics of a good abstract. Is there a trick to putting it all together? Not really, but there is a process you can follow that will yield an effective abstract.

1. Read the article that follows this assignment. Then review the elements of the theoretical abstract above. Write a brief statement based on the article about each of these elements. Continually refer to the article to be sure that you are accurate.
2. Now review the list of information you've compiled and decide whether each point listed is truly essential. Remember the abstract is intended to represent, rather than fully describe.
3. Next try to put the abstracted information together into a logical series of complete sentences. Count the number of words to see how you're doing. Your target is 75-100 words.

4. Revise your draft, attempting to be more concise and specific. Go back to the article for confirmation of what you've written and to be sure you haven't distorted its meaning. You may have to repeat this step several times.
5. When you are satisfied with your draft, check it against the characteristics of a good abstract explained earlier in this chapter.

From Bad to Worth
CHARLES KRAUTHAMMER

The latest entry on the list of sacred Democratic causes is comparable worth. According to that doctrine, it is demonstrable that low-paying female-dominated jobs, like nursing, are worth as much (to employers or society) as "comparable" male-dominated jobs, like plumbing, and that therefore by right and by law they should be paid the same. Comparable worth has become not only *the* women's issue of the 1980s but also the most prominent civil rights issue not specifically directed at blacks. The Democratic Party has warmly embraced it. Every one of its Presidential candidates has endorsed it. In the 1984 platform, that sea of well-intended ambiguity and evasion, there are few islands of certainty. Comparable worth is one of them.

Comparable worth is advancing in the courts, too. Three years ago the Supreme Court opened the door a crack by ruling that female prison guards could sue for violation of the equal-pay provisions of the 1964 Civil Rights Act, even though they did not do precisely the same work as the better-paid male prison guards. That narrow ruling was broken open last December in a sweeping victory for comparable worth in Washington State. A federal district judge found the state guilty of massive discrimination because its female-dominated jobs were paying less than "comparable" male-dominated jobs. He ordered an immediate increase in the women's wages and restitution for past injury. The back pay alone will run into the hundreds of millions of dollars.

Comparable worth may indeed be an idea whose time has come. Where does it come from? When the plumber makes a house call and charges $40 an hour to fix a leak, the instinct of most people is to suspect that the plumber is overpaid — the beneficiary of some combination of scarce skills, powerful unions, and dumb luck. The instinct of comparable worth advocates is to see the plumber's wage as a standard of fairness, to conclude that the rest of us (meaning: women) are underpaid, and to iden-

36

tify discrimination as the source of that underpayment. But since overt discrimination on the basis of sex has been legally forbidden for twenty years, to make that charge stick nowadays requires a bit of subtlety.

One claim is that women's wages are depressed today because of a legacy of past discrimination: namely, the "crowding" of women into certain fields (like nursing, teaching, secretarial work), thus artificially depressing their wages. Did sexual stereotyping really "crowd" women into their jobs? Sexual stereotyping worked both ways: it kept women in, but it also kept men out, thus artificially excluding potential wage competition from half the population, and, more important, from about two-thirds to three-quarters of the labor force (because of the higher participation rate of men). Sex-segregation is obviously unfair, but it is hard to see how it caused downward pressure on women's wages when, at the same time, through the socially enforced exclusion of men, it sheltered "women's work" from a vast pool of competitors. Moreover, as the social barriers that kept men and women from entering each other's traditional fields have fallen during the last twenty years, there has been much more movement of women into men's fields than vice versa. "Women's work" is less crowded than ever.

If the crowding argument is weak, then one is forced to resort to the "grand conspiracy" theory. "The system of wages was set up by a grand conspiracy, so to speak, that has held down the wages of women to minimize labor costs," explained the business agent of the union that in 1981 struck for and won a famous comparable-worth settlement in San Jose. But since to minimize labor costs employers try to hold down the wages of everyone, the thrust of the argument must be that there is a particular desire to do so additionally in the case of women. In other words, the market is inherently discriminatory. Women nurses are paid less than they deserve, simply because they are women. How to prove it? Comparing their wages to that of male nurses won't do, since their pay is, by law, equal. So one must compare nurses' wages to that of, say, plumbers, show that nurses make less, and claim that nurses are discriminated against because they deserve — they are worth — the same.

What is the basis of that claim? In San Jose, Washington State, and other comparable worth cases, the basis is a "study." A consultant is called in to set up a committee to rank every job according to certain criteria. In Washington State, the "Willis" scale gives marks for "knowledge and skills," "mental demands," "accountability," and "working conditions." The committee then awards points in each category to every job, tallies them up, and declares those with equal totals to have — *voila!* — comparable worth.

There is no need to belabor the absurdity of this system, so I'll stick to the high points. It is, above all, a mandate for arbitrariness: every subjective determination, no matter how whimsically arrived at, is first enshrined in a number to give it an entirely specious solidity, then added to another number no less insubstantial, to yield a total entirely meaningless. (An exercise: compare, with numbers, the "mental demands" on a truck driver and a secretary.) Everything is arbitrary: the categories, the rankings, even the choice of judges. And even if none of this were true, even if every category were ontologically self-evident, every ranking mathematically precise, every judge Solomonic, there remains one factor wholly unaccounted for which permits the system to be skewed in any direction one wishes: the *weight* assigned to each category. In the Willis scale, points for "knowledge and skills" are worth as much as points for "working conditions." But does ten points in knowledge and skills make up for ten points in hazardous working conditions? Who is to say that a secretary's two years of college are equal in worth to — and not half or double the worth of — the trucker's risk of getting killed on the highways? Mr. Willis, that's who.

Conclusions based on such "studies" are not a whit less capricious than the simple assertion, "secretaries are worth as much as truck drivers." Trotting out Willis, of course, allows you to dress up a feeling in scientific trappings. It allows H.R. 4599, Representative Mary Rose Oakar's bill legislating comparable worth in federal employment, to dispose of the arbitrariness problem in the *definitions*. "Job evaluation technique" is defined as "an objective method of determining the comparable value of different jobs." Next problem.

Some advocates of comparable worth, aware of this objectivity conundrum and perhaps less confident that it can be defined out of existence, propose an alternate solution. Instead of ranking the intrinsic worth of the job (by admittedly arbitrary criteria), they propose ranking the worth of the worker. Barbara Bergmann, an economist at the University of Maryland, believes that people with similar qualifications, training, and experience should be receiving the same return on their "human capital." Breaking new ground in discrimination theory, she claims that "in a nondiscriminatory setup, identical people should be paid identically." And what makes people identical? Their credentials: qualifications, training, experience. This is not just credentialism gone wild, and highly disadvantageous to non-yuppy workers with poor résumés, who need the help of the women's movement the most; it leads to the logical absurdity that people should be paid not for the actual work they do, but for the work they *could* do. We've gone from equal pay for equal work to equal pay for comparable work, to equal pay for potential work. Summarizing the Bergmann position, the Center for Philosophy in Public Policy at the University of Maryland explains helpfully that "if a nursing supervisor could do the work of a higher-paid hospital purchasing agent, then her wages should be the same as his." But why stop here? What if her credentials are the same as those of the hospital administrator, or her city councillor, or her U.S. Senator? And what about the starving actress, waiting on tables for a living? If she can act as well as Bo Derek (to set a standard anyone can meet), shouldn't she be getting a million dollars a year — that is, if the "setup" is to deserve the adjective "nondiscriminatory"?

Now, even if there were a shred of merit in any of these systems for determining comparable worth, we should be wary of implementing them if only because of the sheer social chaos they would create. The only sure consequence of comparable worth one can foresee was described by the winning attorney in the Washington State case: "This decision . . . should stimulate an avalanche of private litigation on behalf of the victims of discrimination." The judicial and bureaucratic monster comparable worth will call into being — a whole new layer of judges, court-appointed "masters" (there already is one in the Washington State suit), lawyers, and consultants — will not just sit once to fix wages and then retire. The process will be endless. Fairness will require constant readjustment. There will still exist such a thing as supply and demand. Even if comparable worth advocates succeed in abolishing it for women's work (remember, Washington State was found to have broken the law for paying women market wages rather than comparable worth wages), it will still operate for men's wages, the standard by which women's (comparable worth) wages will be set. Now, what if nurses are awarded plumbers' pay, and there develops a housing slowdown and a plumber surplus, and plumbers' wages fall? Will nurses' salaries have to be ratcheted down? And if not, what is to prevent the plumbers from suing, alleging they are underpaid relative to comparably equal nurses?

Which brings us to the equity problem. Almost everyone feels he or she is underpaid. Moreover, even a plumber can point to at least one person or group of persons who are getting more than they are "worth." Why can't he claim that class of people as the equitable standard, and march to court demanding restitution? If comparable worth is simple justice, as its advocates claim, why should only women be entitled to it? Why not comparable worth for everyone?

The whole search for the "just wage," which is what comparable worth is all about, is like the search for the "just price," inherently elusive in a capitalist system. It is not that justice has nothing to say about wages and prices in a market economy, but that what it does say it says negatively.

For example, it declares that whatever the wage, it must be the same for people regardless of sex, race, or other characteristics; but it doesn't say what the wage should be. Even the minimum-wage law says merely that a wage may not be below a certain floor. (Even capitalism has a notion of exploitative labor.) Beyond that, the law is silent. The reason it is silent, the reason we decide to let the market decide, is no great mystery. It was first elaborated by Adam Smith, and amplified by the experience of the Soviet Union and other command economies. Market economies are agnostic on the question of a just wage or a just price not simply because of a philosophical belief that the question, if it is a question, is unanswerable, but also because of the belief, and the experience, that attempts to answer it have a habit of leaving everyone worse off than before.

Finally, even granting that women in traditionally female jobs are underpaid, it is not as if we live in a fixed economy which blocks off all avenues of redress. If secretaries are indeed paid less than they are "worth," they have several options. One is suggested by Coleman Young, the mayor of Detroit, a former labor leader and no conservative: "If a painter makes more than a secretary, then let more women be painters. Equal opportunity and affirmative action is how you do that." A woman entering the labor force today has no claim that she has been crowded into low-paying professions because of discrimination. She has choices.

Older women, of course, who have already invested much in their professions, are more constrained. But they have the same avenues open to them — such as organizing — as other similarly constrained (predominantly male) workers who struggle for higher wages in other settings. In Denver, for example, nurses sought comparable worth wage gains in court and lost; they then went on strike and won. True, in some occupations, even strong unions can't raise wages very much. But as the president of the International Ladies Garment Workers Union (85 percent female) explained in objecting to a highfalutin A.F.L.-C.I.O. endorsement of comparable worth, the problem is not discrimination but the market. His workers have low wages because they compete with workers overseas who are paid thirty cents an hour. Comparable worth doctrine may declare that garment workers ought to be making as much as truck drivers. But if the theory ever became practice, garment workers would be free of more than discrimination. They would be free of their jobs.

Why is the obvious about comparable worth so rarely heard? Why is it for Democrats the ultimate motherhood issue? Because here again the party of the big heart identifies a class of people who feel they aren't getting their just due, blames that condition on a single cause (discrimination), then offers a "rational" solution, on whose messy details it prefers not to

40

dwell. But those details add up to a swamp of mindless arbitrariness and bureaucratic inefficiency, shrouded in a fine mist of pseudo-scientific objectivity. And the surest results will be unending litigation and an entirely new generation of inequities. These inequities, moreover, will be frozen in place by force of law, and thus that much more difficult to dislodge.

Comparable worth asks the question: How many nurses would it take to screw in a lightbulb? The joke is that, having not the faintest idea, it demands that a committee invent an answer, that the answer become law, and that the law supplant the market. Even Karl Marx, who also had legitimate complaints about the equity of wages set by the market, had a more plausible alternative.

Book Review

Reading book reviews is one way that professional political scientists keep up with their fields. It's also an excellent method for the student of political science to sample the range of current theory and research. Reviews of political science books appear in serious magazines like *Harpers* and the *Atlantic* and in book review journals like the *New York Times Book Review* and the *New York Review of Books*. But they can be found in far greater numbers in scholarly journals like *Comparative Political Studies* and the *American Political Science Review*. One recent issue of the latter journal contained ninety-seven pages of reviews!

Reading book reviews is one thing, writing them is another. Because the assignment to write a book review exposes the student to the primary literature in the field, it is common not only in political science courses but also in psychology, education, history, and many other disciplines. Although the specifics of the assignment may vary, professors usually want to help you develop analytical skills in reading, to give you practice in presenting main ideas and supporting them with a line of reasoning, and to encourage you to make a critical assessment of the book.

A good book review for a political science course should

1. Identify the book completely: author or editor, full title, publisher, and place and date of publication.
2. Describe the subject and scope of the book.

41

3. Give information about the author, focusing on his or her qualifications for writing this book. (Ask the reference librarian for help in finding this information.)
4. Outline or summarize the thrust or argument of the book, giving the main pieces of evidence to support author's position.
5. Tell whether, in your judgment, the author satisfactorily supports the thesis or argument.
6. Connect the book to the larger world by explaining the ramifications of the argument or material, by assessing the value of the book, or by placing it in the context of public issues or of other current books on the subject.
7. Relate the book's subject or thesis to the academic course.

WRITING 3.2: READING A BOOK REVIEW. Read the review of *The Supreme Court and Constitutional Democracy* that follows. As you read, look for the elements of a good book review explained above and mark them in the margins. For instance, mark with the number 2 the paragraph or sentence where the reviewer describes the subject and scope of the book. Also jot down responses to these questions: Are any of the elements omitted? Can you think of reasons for the omission? Which of the elements receive the most extensive treatment? Can you suggest why? This work should give you a better idea of the way one reviewer, at least, fulfilled his obligations to his readers.

The Supreme Court and Constitutional Democracy. By John Agresto. (Ithaca, N.Y.: Cornell University Press, 1984. Pp. 182. $25.00, cloth; $7.95, paper.)

CHRISTOPHER WOLFE

Marquette University

John Agresto has written a book that tries to provide an outline for a new solution to the perennial problem of judicial review and democracy. "How," he asks, "do we, as a nation, give the Court the power and opportunity to guide us through our living and developing Constitution and still prevent the Court from substituting its principles of the Constitution, and elevating its rule over ours? In that question is the whole tangled problem this book has sought to unroll" (p. 160).

Agresto makes use of historical analysis of the origin and growth of judicial review to present a picture of an early judicial review deeply rooted in the principle of separation of powers. With Lincoln he deplores the emergence of the notion that judicial interpretation of the Constitution is final and binding on the other branches. Calling for a restoration of checks on the Court, he defends the effectiveness of Congress' power to ask the Court to reconsider its decisions (especially when supported by the force of public and scholarly opinion and timely use of the appointment power). Yet, apparently sensing the inadequacy of such checks, Agresto calls for scholars to consider how they may be used more effectively.

The last chapter elaborates more fully the two goods Agresto wants to achieve at the same time. The Court is called upon to fulfill an important role in our society: not just checking legislation, but investigating questions of political and moral philosophy, fostering the growth of evolving national principles. At the same time, this must not be permitted to yield judicial oligarchy, especially with the developing power of the courts to give affirmative commands. "Checked activism" is the *via media* whereby these twin goals are to be achieved.

But "checked activism" is not the answer, in my opinion. The reasons why are hinted at in Agresto's own ambivalent attitude toward the Framers. He clearly has a high regard for them — no work is cited more often than *The Federalist*. But ultimately, he departs from their understanding of judicial power. His most frequent citation to describe the "activism" side of his "checked activism" is to Alexander Bickel, who expressly rejected *Marbury v. Madison* as too narrow a rationale. Like Bickel, but unlike the Founders I think, Agresto argues that the judiciary has been entrusted with the task of developing our evolving ideals and principles, seeing in them implications which the Framers did not have sufficient foresight to see. Perhaps it is not surprising, then, that Agresto implicitly criticizes the Framers for not attaching more effective checks to the judiciary (e.g., allowing an extraordinary congressional majority to override an exercise of judicial review). The Framers did not need such a check because they provided for a more limited judicial power, which would employ judicial review simply to enforce clear constitutional commands. I think that the Framers would have been rightly suspicious of whether "checked activism" would be sufficiently checked.

But my concerns about the solution proposed by this book should not obscure its considerable merit. *The Supreme Court and Constitutional Democracy* deals with a question which is the permanent question about national judicial power in America, and it makes a substantial contribution to our contemporary discussion by reminding us of the context of judicial review as it was originally conceived: separation of powers and checks and balances. Only relatively recently in American history has the notion of the finality of Court interpretations ("the Constitution is what the judges say it is") become so widespread, and Agresto's book shows why this view is such an unfortunate one. If it is not successful in its attempt to attain the best of both worlds (constitutional restraint and judicial activism), it does focus our attention on the wisdom of the founding, which may point us in the right direction.

WRITING 3.3: WRITING A BOOK REVIEW. Choose a recent book within the scope of this course (your professor may provide a list of titles or direct you to the suggestions for further reading in your textbook). Before you read the book, review the guidelines given earlier. Knowing what you are looking for will help you read faster and more effectively. When you write your review, refer to the guidelines frequently, but don't follow them slavishly. Let your own response to the book show through.

LEARNING TO SYNTHESIZE

When you were in sixth or seventh grade, you probably had to write a report on Peru or whales or the Battle of Bunker Hill. Remember how you went to the encyclopedia and sort of summarized the article? Your creative contribution was limited to the choice of crayon color for the cover and yarn for the binding. A few years later, more sophisticated, you summarized three or four articles when you had to write a report, or paper, as it was more likely called. You might have rearranged the material a little and even added a bibliography, but contributed little more.

As you now know, that wasn't research. Library research involves a good deal of reading (and note-taking) from various sources and the even more difficult task of thinking about that information, making sense of it somehow. Relating ideas from several sources, adding your insights, viewing the topic from your own, perhaps newly discovered, perspective — these intellectual processes can lead to a **synthesis**, a combining of parts to produce a whole. More than the sum of its sources, the synthesis you produce from your thinking and reading is a new vision of the topic or issue. And that is what your professor will be looking for in the work you do.

WRITING 3.4: THE ONE-PARAGRAPH RESEARCH ESSAY.   Your task is to explore a fairly complex subject in a one-paragraph research essay. Taking notes on your reading, developing a thesis, organizing and synthesizing ideas, and documenting your sources are all necessary.

At the end of these instructions, you'll find a list of articles and judicial opinions treating the issue of affirmative action. These are the only sources you'll need. Begin by reading them all to get a feeling for the topic, making notes on important points. Realize that you cannot summarize all of this information in a single paragraph. That's not the point. The point is to develop a clearly defined perspective on the issue (in the form of a summary or an argument), illustrating or proving it with material from at least four of these sources. To do this you'll need to synthesize or put together material from several authors and arrange it into logical subtopics. You should include quotation, paraphrase, and summary as explained in Chapter 7. Credit your sources and add a list of works cited according to the rules outlined in Chapter 8. (This assignment is based on the work of Susan Peck MacDonald of Eastern Connecticut State College.)

The Sources (Not necessarily in the correct form. See Chapter 8):

1. Justice Thurgood Marshall, dissenting opinion, *Regents of the University of California vs. Allan Bakke,* 438 U.S. 265 (1978), 387–402.
2. Justice Potter Stewart, dissenting opinion, *Fullilove vs. Klutznick,* 448 U.S. 448 (1978), 522–532.
3. Morris B. Abram, "What Constitutes a Civil Right?" *The New York Times Magazine* (June 10, 1984).

4. Sidney Hook, "The Tyranny of Reverse Discrimination," *Change*, December-January, 1975–1976.
5. Rose Laub Coser, "Affirmative Action: Letter to a Worried Colleague," *Dissent*, Fall 1975.
6. Maguire, Daniel, "Quotas: Unequal But Fair." *Commonweal*, October 14, 1977.

UNDERSTANDING CONTEMPORARY AFFAIRS

The newest textbook you own is at least one year old. That's how long it takes a publisher to edit, print, and distribute a book after receiving the manuscript. There's no telling how long the author labored over the research and writing. Thus the citizen who is concerned about current events must turn to newspapers, news magazines, and other sources to keep up with today's developments in government, politics, and foreign affairs. This is how members of the State Department and other government agencies keep abreast of what is happening in the world. Of the hundreds of periodicals published in the United States daily, only a few are so widely read and respected as to form the core of common reading of the nation's leaders and policy makers. These are the newspapers and magazines the student of political science should know and read regularly:

Newsweek

Time

U.S. News and World Report

Christian Science Monitor

Los Angeles Times

New York Times

Washington Post

WRITING 3.5: THE CLIPPING THESIS. Many political science instructors use current events to illustrate important concerns of their discipline. As a student of political science, you will find that regular reading of a national newspaper or news magazine will help you to understand your subject. For this writing, follow for a period of time the development of a current issue, collecting articles from one or more of the sources named above. At the end of the period of study, you will use the clippings to write an analysis of the issue.

Steps:

1. Choose an issue of public policy relevant to your course of study. Example: for a course in international relations, the topic of arms limitation negotiations between the United States and the Union of Soviet Socialist Republics. Example: for a course in American government, the issue of comparable worth.
2. Read your source regularly and clip or photocopy articles relating to your issue. Write your reactions to them in your journal.
3. Based on your file, write an analysis explaining the origins and development of the topic, the political and governmental processes involved, the status of the issue at the end of the study, and likely future development of the issue.

(This assignment is based on the work of Professor William Rogers, State University of New York at Cortland.)

Pointers for Your Written Analysis:

1. Reference every clipping (source, date, page number) according to the guidelines in Chapter 7.
2. Include in your analysis at least one quotation, one paraphrase, and one summary. Reference these according to the guidelines in Chapter 7.
3. Feel free to use additional sources (e.g., textbooks, reference works) for background on the issue. Credit these sources as shown in Chapters 7 and 8.

EXPRESSING AN OPINION

Citizens participate in politics in many ways other than voting. They read newspapers, watch television news and documentaries, join politically active associations, contribute money, time, and effort to political campaigns, discuss politics with others, telephone governmental bureaucrats with complaints, and write letters to newspaper editors and public officials.

Letters to the Editor

Letters to the editor often serve a dual purpose. They are "open letters" addressed both to a particular official and to the public. The purpose is not only to express your opinion on an issue, but also to change the views of the readers. Letters written solely to get something off your chest are seldom effective.

Although editors print only some of the correspondence they receive, if your letter is well written and thoughtful your chances of publication are very good. Newspapers allot limited space to "letters to the editor," so the first rule is to be brief. Seventy-five to two hundred words is an appropriate length. Organize the letter carefully. One kind of letter to the editor is really a condensed argument (see Chapter 4), and contains the following elements:

1. Statement of the issue.
2. Presentation of factual, noncontroversial background information the reader needs to understand the issue.
3. Statement of writer's position on the issue.
4. Presentation of evidence and/or reasoning to support writer's position.
5. Refutation of opponents' arguments.
6. Conclusion and a call to action.

Elements 4 and 5 are sometimes reversed. Here is a letter to the editor of *The New York Times* on the subject of campaign financing:

Don't Let the President Kill the $1 Checkoff

To the Editor:

If Congress isn't careful, President Reagan will wipe out one of the most important campaign reforms of the past two decades.

Every year, tens of millions of Americans check off $1 of their Federal income tax payment to provide public financing of Presidential campaigns. The result: candidates are far less dependent on big business and other special interests to run an effective race.

But if President Reagan has his way, the $1 checkoff will be repealed to eliminate what the White House calls "a source of confusion" for taxpayers: With that, public funding for Presidential campaigns would end unless Congress and the President were to agree on a new plan — which a Federal Election Commission spokesman termed, in light of the deficit crisis, "nigh unto impossible."

Presidential candidates who accept Federal campaign funds must agree to limit total expenditures and contributions from other sources. Without public funding, we will once again see fat cats shoveling cash at candidates, who will be expected to return favors after taking office.

Besides the $1 checkoff, the President's tax return plan would eliminate the $50 credit taxpayers can now receive for contributions to political candidates and political action committees. Contrary to occasional criticisms, this credit is used not just by the rich but by all income groups. Treasury Department figures show that more than 45 percent of the tax benefit from the credit goes to those with incomes of less than $30,000. Eliminating it would only lessen average Americans' say in the selection of those who run their Government.

Ironically, President Reagan knows the value of the $1 checkoff better than anyone, having collected a total of more than $90 million from the Federal Election Commission — more than any other candidate — in the three Presidential election years since such financing became available. Now that he has used the system fully and cannot run again, does the President want to pull the ladder up behind him? That isn't fair to George Bush, Gary Hart and others who hope to occupy the White House someday.

More importantly, it is an attack on a system that has gone a long way toward restoring integrity and public confidence in our Presidential election process. Congress must make sure that attack fails.

Arthur J. Kremer
Albany, Sept. 19, 1985

The writer is chairman of the New York State Assembly Ways and Means Committee.

WRITING 3.6: READING A LETTER TO THE EDITOR. Analyze Kremer's letter to the editor by looking for the elements of an argument listed earlier. When you find each element, mark it. For instance, mark with the number 1 the sentence or paragraph where Kremer states the issue. Are any of the elements omitted? Which of the elements receive the most extensive treatment? Why do you suppose Kremer did this? What function do the author's credentials play in the matter?

WRITING 3.7: WRITING A LETTER TO THE EDITOR. It's your turn. Choose one of the options below and draft a letter to the editor. Follow the format of an argument outlined earlier. Be aware of your two audiences and identify clearly the official or officials to whom your argument is ultimately addressed. Try to keep your letter under 250 words.

A. Select an issue affecting life on your campus and write a letter to the editor of your student newspaper.
B. Select an issue in the national political spotlight and write a letter to the editor of your local newspaper.

Letters to Public Officials

More direct than a letter to the editor is to write to public officials themselves, avoiding intermediaries such as newspaper editors. Government officials who commonly receive letters from constituents and persons affected by their decisions include mayors, city council members, heads of departments, boards, authorities and commissions, state and federal legislators, governors, and even the President. It is considered improper to write a judge in an attempt to influence the decision in a pending case but it is perfectly proper to write to your congressman in an effort to influence his or her vote on a piece of pending legislation. There is evidence that policy makers, especially elected ones, pay heed to their mail and that letter-writing can be an effective means of making government accountable to the people. The names and addresses of members of the federal legislative, executive, and judicial branches can be found in the *United States Government Manual,* updated and published each year. In such a letter, your goal is to persuade the reader to do or omit some action. Use the same format that you would use in writing a letter to the editor.

WRITING 3.8: ANALYZING A LETTER. Analyze the following letter from a student organization to the president of the faculty senate. In the margins, write the number corresponding to the outline elements listed earlier next to where these elements occur in the letter. What pending action is the author seeking to influence?

```
Professor Gordon Stone
President
Faculty Senate

Dear Professor Stone:
     The faculty next week will be voting on a res-
olution to ban all defense-related research at this
university. The College Republicans, a student po-
litical organization, strongly oppose this proposed
resolution. We understand that the proponents re-
gard university research on the President's Stra-
tegic Defense Initiative and other defense-related
projects as immoral. The moral argument in favor of
such research is much stronger, however, than the
moral argument against it.
     Advocates of a ban on defense-related research
profess a strong belief in academic freedom. Such
freedom exists, however, only in a free society.
Therefore, those who are committed to academic
freedom have a moral obligation to defend a free
society when a tyrannical enemy threatens it. There
is no academic freedom in the Soviet Union. If pro-
fessors there attempted to boycott any class of
government-sponsored research, they would join An-
drei Sakharov in internal exile or become inmates
in mental hospitals or the Gulag. No universities
banned defense-related research during the Nazi
threat. University-affiliated scientists, in fact,
enthusiastically worked to develop the atomic bomb
to respond to this threat. The Soviet Union is a
much more formidable enemy of the United States
than Germany ever was. Marxism-Leninism demands the
destruction of the "capitalistic and imperialistic"
United States. Neither the theory nor the prac-
tice of communism gives us any hope for an end to
Soviet-American hostility.
     Although the "peace-loving" Soviets talk of
the need for disarmament, they have threatened
China explicitly with nuclear annihilation. Scien-
tists in the U.S.S.R. are working diligently to de-
```

velop their own "Star Wars" capability, and if such research were to stop here they would be the only ones with this capability.

The alternative to defense research being conducted in universities is for it to be done by the military in secret laboratories. One of the hallmarks of American defense-related research is civilian domination. Civilian control of the military is one of our fundamental constitutional principles and is necessary to ensure against coups d'état, common in much of the rest of the world.

It is unfair for a majority of the faculty to prohibit those scholars and scientists who wish to do such research from accepting support from the Department of Defense. No one is forcing individual faculty members who have scruples about Star Wars to accept grants to conduct such research. No one is pressuring them to approve U.S. foreign or defense policy. Because of academic freedom, faculty members are free to speak out against government policy.

Many of the faculty engaged in defense research are patriotic citizens who have chosen to use their talents to help defend the free world. This proposed ban would make them appear to be accomplices in evil.

We all wish to avert a nuclear catastrophe. The President's Strategic Defense Initiative is well designed to minimize the ability of the Soviets to destroy U.S. cities. By obstructing Star Wars and other defense research, proponents of the ban are increasing the likelihood of a world where faculty no longer have the freedom to object to foreign policy decisions. On behalf of the College Republicans, I strongly oppose the proposed resolution and urge the faculty to defeat it. Would you bring our views to their attention?

> Sincerely yours,
> Sarah Bauer
> President
> College Republicans

WRITING 3.9: LETTER TO A PUBLIC OFFICIAL I.

Write a letter to a campus official on an issue that concerns you. Be sure to indicate precisely what you want that official to do.

> WRITING 3.10: LETTER TO A PUBLIC OFFICIAL II.
> Write a letter to your congressman in the U.S. House of Representatives. Consult a recent issue of *Congressional Quarterly Weekly Report,* choose a bill pending before the House, and write a letter calling upon your representative to vote either for or against it.

READING FOR MAIN IDEAS, WRITING TO SUMMARIZE (II)

Earlier in this chapter we explored the skills required in reading for main ideas and writing to summarize. The summary, the abstract, and the book review all depend on those skills. Yet another type of writing assignment calls for the same abilities — the legal brief.

Briefing Court Decisions

In a number of political science courses students read the opinions of courts of appeal, usually those of the United States Supreme Court. Undergraduates rarely are asked to study the decisions and orders of trial court judges. A useful device for analyzing and summarizing appellate court decisions is the brief. A brief is similar to an abstract, but the main ideas you are searching for are rules of law established by the court. Writing a brief provides you the opportunity to distill the court's opinion into its essentials, to separate the wheat from the chaff of judicial exposition. In courses such as constitutional law, where you must read many cases, briefs become indispensable study aids. Learning to brief cases is also excellent preparation for law school.

A brief is about 400 words long and consists of six parts:

1. Name and citation
2. Key facts
3. The issue
4. Holding and vote
5. Reasoning of the majority
6. Separate opinions

Let's examine each of these parts by studying a sample brief of the landmark school desegregation case, *Brown v. Board of Education.*

```
1.  NAME AND CITATION
Brown v. Board of Education of Topeka, 347 U.S. 483
(1954).
```

Comment:

The name of the person appealing the lower court's decision, the **appellant**, precedes the name of his or her adversary, the victor in the lower court, the **appellee.** Law suits are adversary proceedings; thus we place a *v.* for *versus* between the names of the parties. Because the lower courts upheld Topeka's right to separate children in public schools according to race, Linda Brown's appeal to the U.S. Supreme Court is known as *Brown v. Board of Education of Topeka.* Immediately following the case name is its citation. This tells the reader where the full opinion can be found. The *Brown* decision can be located in volume 347 of the *United States Reports* beginning on page 483. The citation also includes the year in which the court handed down its decision.

```
2.  KEY FACTS
Linda Brown, a Negro minor, was denied admission to
a school attended by white children under a law of
the state of Kansas permitting segregation accord-
ing to race. Through her legal representative,
Linda Brown seeks the aid of the courts in obtain-
ing admission to the public schools of her commu-
nity on a nonsegregated basis.
```

Comment:

When making their decisions, judges apply the relevant law to the facts of the particular case. The object in part 2 is to present the key facts: i.e., the facts that determine the court's decision. Your summary of the material facts should be no more than 150 words.

```
3.  THE ISSUE
Does legally-imposed segregation of children in
public schools solely on the basis of race, even
though physical facilities may be equal, deprive
```

```
the minority children of "the equal protection of
the laws," guaranteed by section 1 of the Four-
teenth Amendment?
```

Comment:

As we have seen, judicial decisions are the product of the law and
the facts. In a brief the writer introduces the relevant law in the
form of a legal question or issue. The issue must be stated as a one-
sentence question that can be answered yes or no. Because many
Supreme Court decisions require interpretation of the Constitution,
the issue is often a constitutional question. Be careful to specify the
particular article or amendment and section or clause of the Constitution in dispute.

```
4.  HOLDING AND VOTE
Yes (vote 9-0) (Opinion by Chief Justice Warren).
```

Comment:

The holding of the court is its resolution of the issue, either yes or
no. Because appellate courts are collegial bodies, unlike trial courts
over which a single judge typically presides, decisions are reached
by a show of hands. You will find in the reports an indication of
how each member of the court voted. Note how many answered
yes and how many no to the legal question. Also tell who wrote the
opinion for the majority.

```
5.  REASONING
Segregated schools can never provide Negroes with
equal educational opportunities, even if the Negro
and white schools are equal in buildings, curri-
cula, qualifications and salaries of teachers, and
other "tangible" factors. Such segregation of white
and black children in public schools has a detri-
mental effect upon the black children, an impact
that is greater when it has the sanction of the
law. It "generates a feeling of inferiority as to
their status in the community that may affect their
hearts and minds in a way unlikely ever to be un-
done." Studies by Dr. Kenneth Clark and other so-
cial pscyhologists show conclusively that racial
```

segregation adversely affects the self-concept, mo-
tivation, and achievement of Negro children. "Separate educational facilities are inherently unequal.
Therefore, we hold that the [appellant] and others
similarly situated for whom the actions have been
brought are, by reason of the segregation com-
plained of, deprived of the equal protection of the
laws guaranteed by the Fourteenth Amendment."

Comment:

Unlike executives and legislators, judges must give reasons justifying their decisions. Because future courts, under the rule of prece-
dent, must decide cases presenting the same factual and legal situ-
ations as past cases, the higher court's rationale provides lower
courts, as well as the public, with critical legal guidance. Your summary of the reasoning of the majority of the court justifying its
holding is the most important part of the brief. You must confine
your summary to the essential reasons and omit all *obiter dicta*,
statements that are not necessary for the decision of the case. The
reasoning section should not exceed 200 words. Be sure to place in
quotation marks any passages drawn directly from the text of the
opinion.

        6. SEPARATE OPINIONS
        None.

Comment:

Those judges who disagree with the majority can file separate opinions. If the judge agrees with the court's holding but not with its
reasoning, he or she can write a concurring opinion, explaining
why the reasoning is inadequate. If the judge voted to decide the
case differently, he or she can submit a dissenting opinion, explaining why the court's holding is erroneous. In a brief the writer usually only mentions any separate opinions and does not summarize
them. This is because only the majority opinion, or opinion of the
court, has the force of law. Because the *Brown* opinion was unan-
imous, there are no separate opinions, and you would place a
"none" in part 6. In *Milliken v. Bradley, 418 U.S. 717 (1974)*, however, a sharply divided Supreme Court held 5-4 that a desegregation

plan that bused black children from Detroit into the white suburbs could not be sustained under the Fourteenth Amendment's equal protection clause. In your brief of the *Milliken* case, you would provide the following information in section 6:

(a) Justice White wrote a dissenting opinion, which was joined by Justices Marshall, Brennan, and Douglas.
(b) Justice Marshall wrote a dissenting opinion, which was joined by Justices White, Brennan, and Douglas.
(c) Justice Douglas wrote a dissenting opinion.

WRITING 3.11: BRIEFING A SUPREME COURT DECISION. Select a Supreme Court decision that interests you and write a brief. Follow the guidelines given above and limit yourself to 400 words.

[4] *Issues and Arguments*

PREVIEW: *Politics means controversy. In this chapter you will learn how to analyze controversial issues and how to present persuasive arguments.*
Why use this method?
First stage: choosing an issue
Second stage: analyzing an issue
Third stage: taking a stand on an issue

Politics, like the weather and unlike organic chemistry, is one of those subjects on which everyone seems to have an opinion. Raise a political issue among your friends, and you are sure to start an argument. "What business does the United States have meddling in Central America?" "Shouldn't all the nuclear power plants be shut down?" "Isn't the death penalty uncivilized?"

You, of course, would like to win these contests. In this chapter you will learn a method for preparing more effective arguments. The final product is an issue analysis, which can be submitted as a term paper or be the basis of an oral presentation or formal debate. If you are considering law as a career, you will be interested in knowing that the political argument is similar to a kind of writing frequently assigned by law school professors — the attorney's brief. Lawyers represent clients, who often become parties to lawsuits. During the trial, the attorney's task is to advocate the interests of the client by making the strongest possible argument in his or her behalf. Lawyers have learned that the best prepared advocate is one who can argue the opposition's case better than the opposition can. This principle holds for winning debates over controversial political issues as well as for winning trials.

Recall that the writing process consists of three stages: prewriting, drafting and rewriting. In the prewriting stage described below, you will select an issue of current interest, sharpen your focus, conduct research, and write a balanced analysis of your issue.

Only then will you be ready for the drafting stage, in which you will write an essay arguing one side of the question you selected in stage one. During the final, or rewriting, phase you will ask others to read your work and suggest improvements before revising your draft.

WHY USE THIS METHOD?

The sequence of tasks is designed to help you acquire a number of attitudes and abilities, both general ones and those associated with success in the study of political science, and develop facility in argumentation. The general skills the sequence will help you master are

> to use library resources
>
> to weigh the bias and reliability of a source
>
> to distinguish statements of fact from opinions or preferences
>
> to base judgment on knowledge
>
> to synthesize information.

The particular political science skills this sequence will help you learn are

> to define a political issue as a question that can be studied and answered
>
> to understand that a policy question has two sides
>
> to become well informed before taking a position on an issue
>
> to appreciate that politics involves action as well as thought.

Students who try the process approach prefer it over the traditional "night before" method for a number of reasons. In the first place, they find it easier to meet the instructor's deadline. Because you have to meet a variety of prewriting and drafting deadlines, you are well prepared to complete the final draft on time. Secondly, the grades on these papers are usually higher than those received on term papers done in the old way. One political science professor reported a significant improvement in grades when students employed the process approach.

These are the steps you will be following. You will find explanations for each step and illustrations of student writing. At the end of the chapter is an easy-to-follow outline of the sequence.

FIRST STAGE: CHOOSING AN ISSUE

Step 1. Write a list of four or five controversial issues related to your course. Where are good places to find relevant issues? Course readings and lectures are rich sources. Periodicals, including news magazines, newspapers, and scholarly journals, will also prove helpful. Specialized periodicals are published in each of the major subdisciplines of political science — American politics, political theory, comparative politics, international relations, and political behavior. See Chapter 7 for a list of the major journals in each subdiscipline.

Step 2. Share and discuss your list with others. Why is each issue significant? What is your interest in the issue? How is the issue related to this particular course? Discussion with your classmates will help you explore these questions.

Step 3. Choose one issue and write freely for five minutes about what you know and don't know about the issue. You will want to do a good deal of thinking about your issue. To aid this activity, you will be asked at a couple of points to engage in discovery writing. Discovery writing is a way of thinking on paper, composed for your own needs and not directed to an audience. Don't worry about writing in complete sentences or correct grammar and spelling. You are thinking "aloud," not communicating to others. This early discovery writing will help you explore your understanding of the issue. Some students begin with a personal concern about a problem, then explore that concern for a suitable issue, as this student did with the Equal Rights Amendment:

```
Although I'm a woman and equality of our rights is
extremely important to me, I can't say I know much
about the Equal Rights Amendment. Maybe because the
necessary number of states have refused to ratify
it, maybe because the Reagan administration won't
deal with it; I'm not sure why, but I should know
more about it. . . . My biggest personal concern
about the Equal Rights Amendment isn't so much its
content or its wording, but what implications it
```

```
will have. So much of the Constitution and its
Amendments are left vague and open to wide inter-
pretation and I'm sure the ERA will be no excep-
tion. Of utmost importance is whether adoption of
the ERA will lead to the drafting of women in case
of war.
```
                                                    — Amy Klausner

The writer's indecision and frankness ("I can't say . . . ," "I'm not sure why . . . ," "I'm sure . . .") is typical of writer-based discovery writing. Amy understands that the purpose of this exercise is to explore her concern about an issue. She is writing for herself to herself; the indecision that might be the mark of weakness in a finished paper is appropriate here. Her discovery writing leads her to formulate the issue "Should Congress and the state legislatures ratify the Equal Rights Amendment?"

Discovery writing also can help you to narrow an issue. Here is how one student refined his topic as he thought about it on paper:

```
The issue I will talk about is one that has some-
thing to do with plea bargaining. Only it is on the
juvenile side of the coin. The fact is plea bar-
gaining for juveniles doesn't seem to me to be a
great issue because of the fact that after 21 years
of age records are wiped clean. The maximum sen-
tence for murder for a juvenile is detainment in a
juvenile facility until age 21. If tried as an
adult, the person could face a maximum sentence of
25 years in prison. I think that an interesting is-
sue is one that has something to do with the great
disparity in juvenile punishment and adult punish-
ment. I would like to learn more about this in some
way.
```
                                                    — David Nadel

During the course of his writing, David shifts from a focus on plea bargaining to the issue of equity in the punishment of juvenile and adult offenders. He has come to grips with his issue and moved much closer to formulating it as a question. In the next step, he does just that. His question becomes "Should juvenile criminals be treated the same as adults?"

Still a third use to which students put the discovery writing is to find out what they don't know. Like many researchers, these writers begin with questions and a desire to learn more about their subject:

> Do immigrants have the same rights as an American-
> born citizen? Who are immigrants, illegal aliens,
> people who are citizens of other countries or per-
> haps dual citizens? What should be done with the
> children of illegal aliens that have been born in
> this country? What are the present policies on is-
> sues dealing with illegal aliens? Do illegal aliens
> have the same rights in a court of law as citizens?
> How hard is it to trace the influx of people into
> the U.S.? What are the criteria used in deciding
> the status of an immigrant? Can the use of illegal
> aliens be beneficial to our economy? Is it fair to
> citizens if they can?
>
> — Paul Marad

Through this brief, expressive writing, you will be able to discover an issue of interest to you. It will help you narrow your focus to a manageable aspect of that issue. And you will begin to identify gaps in your knowledge of the issue, good preparation for the research stage of this sequence.

Step 4. Frame your issue as a question (e.g., Should handguns be banned?). Before you can engage in a pro-contra examination of a significant issue, you must define an issue appropriate for such examination. An issue suited to this dialectical approach must be (1) important, (2) controversial, (3) two sided, and (4) serious. You will want to avoid issues that are too general, are too specific, or deal with topics outside the purview of the course. Here are some examples of issues that students found unworkable as first stated and their revisions:

Too broad:	"Are criminals getting justice in the American court system?"
Revision:	"Should plea bargaining be abolished?"

Too broad:	"Should there be stricter laws concerning immigration?"
Revision:	"Should illegal aliens be granted amnesty?"
Too broad:	"Do citizens have the right to interfere in federal government policies managing the use of nuclear power, wastes and arms?"
Revision:	"Should the Diablo Canyon nuclear power plant be permitted to go on line?"
Too narrow:	"Does the death penalty deter murder?"
Revision:	"Should the death penalty be abolished?" Now the student was free to explore the constitutional and moral as well as the behavioral dimensions of the controversy.

SECOND STAGE: ANALYZING AN ISSUE

Step 5. Research the issue you've chosen. See Chapter 7 for suggestions on how to go about gathering the information you will need to write the analysis, draft, and paper.

Step 6. Write a balanced analysis, but do not take a position. The issue analysis is the first major written undertaking in the sequence. It consists of these sections:

1. Context
2. Summary of Pro and Con Arguments
3. Who Makes These Arguments and Why
4. List of Some Specific Actions
5. References

Context

In this part of the analysis, you will provide two kinds of information: a summary of the issue's history and statements of fact that both sides accept. For example, the Context page of one student's analysis of whether the 21-year-old federal drinking age law should be repealed begins:

> Over the past few years, there has been a surge of awareness involving the problems of alcohol. In

64

1982 a law was passed that gave extra funds to any
state that raised its drinking age to 21. Only four
states responded. At the beginning of this year,
the Presidential Commission on drunk driving researched the issue and recommended a uniform national minimum drinking age of 21 in order to help
battle the drunk driving epidemic.

— Lesley Kachadorian

Here the student begins to trace the history of the issue, making the
point that the present debate is the ramification of a movement to
reduce the social costs of alcohol consumption. The example is also
a good one because the writer lays out uncontroverted facts that
are admitted by both sides, such as only four states responded to
Congress' 1982 initiative. Writing good context summaries can
help you distinguish between facts and opinions disguised as facts.

Summary of Pro and Con Arguments

The challenge of this task is to digest partisan essays, to identify the
major arguments in them, and to state each argument in one or two
sentences. The exercise advances understanding because you must
put the arguments of others in your own words. The best summa-
tions are both concise and thorough. Here is an excerpt from an
analysis of the controversy over involuntary civil commitment of
the mentally ill:

List of Con Arguments:

1. Involuntary commitment is punishment without
   trial, imprisonment without time limit, and
   stigmatization without the hope of redress.
2. Being potentially dangerous is not a crime, and
   psychiatrists cannot predict violent behavior.
3. Involuntary commitment violates the Fifth
   Amendment right to refusal on grounds of self-
   incrimination by forcing one to be interviewed
   by a psychiatrist.
4. Involuntary confinement for ''mental illness''

is a deprivation of liberty, which violates
basic human rights guaranteed by the U.S.
Constitution.

5. Mental institutions are not giving the so-
called mentally ill appropriate treatment once
involuntarily institutionalized.

6. The process of involuntary commitment is
arbitrary.

— Patti Cohen

The student made a similar list of Pro Arguments.

Who Makes These Arguments and Why

The purpose of this exercise is to assist you to read critically. You
will begin to realize that, although some advocates are motivated
by a love of justice and the public good, others are moved by self-
interest or the interest of a group which they represent. You can
pursue this kind of information by examining biographies of the
authors in *Who's Who* and other reference books. Here a student
addresses the debate over the future of boxing by identifying the
major opponents of a ban on the sport and offering reasons for
their opposition.

Boxers: They point to the freedom to pursue one's
occupation. A primary motive is money.

Promoters and the Media: Boxing is an important
source of revenues.

Fans: They want to continue to enjoy their favor-
ite sport.

Some Social Scientists: Boxing permits spectators
to release aggression vicariously.

Conservatives: They are opposed in principle to
government interference in sports.

— Lisa Marcoux

Notice that Lisa shows an awareness of interest, one of the key
concepts in the understanding of politics. She recognizes, for instance, that a ban on boxing would be detrimental to the financial
interests of the broadcasting media, one of the wealthiest and most
powerful forces in the shaping of public opinion. The writer, however, does not distinguish among three kinds of motive: principle,
paternalism, and self-interest. She thus places the opposition of po-

66

litical conservatives on the same plane as the opposition of therapists concerned about the mental health of the population and the opposition of promoters concerned about their own pocketbooks. Lisa is clearly aware, nevertheless, that not everyone who advocates a position is moved by a love of justice and the public good.

List of Some Specific Actions

The advocates are attempting not only to convince the reader of the truth of their opinions but also persuade the audience to take some specific action. While looking for such counsel, you will come to appreciate the element of persuasion common to statements on controversial issues. Many essays opposed to forced busing to achieve racial balance, for instance, admonish Congress to propose a constitutional amendment prohibiting the practice and to provide funds for alternative desegregation remedies, such as voluntary transfer programs for inner-city schools in lieu of busing. Many opponents of abortion are working to amend the Constitution and to elect conservatives to political office. You may wish to identify organizations to which a partisan could write for more information and groups that a sympathetic citizen could join. A student writing on the subject of the power of the courts to remove children from their homes suggested that people opposed to this sweeping power write to Parents Anonymous, the Committee for the Rights of Children and Families, and the American Civil Liberties Union.

References

This section also helps develop critical thinking. Eight references, four or so on each side, is about the minimum acceptable number. You will identify each article or book as "Pro," "Con," or "Context," depending on the author's purpose and point of view. See Chapter 9 for help in putting your references in the correct bibliographic form. An analysis of whether eyewitness testimony should be banned from criminal trials as inherently unreliable contains these entries, among others:

    Bazelon, D. L. (1980, March). Eyewitless news. Psy-
        chology Today, 13, 102. (Pro)

Moore, G. (1983, September). Good witnesses don't
    see all. Psychology Today, 17, 5. (Context)
Trankell, A. (1972). Reliability of evidence.
    Stockholm, Sweden: Rotobeckman Press. (Con)
— Donna Toman

Step 7. Show your analysis to others. Ask them if it is thorough and gives adequate treatment to each side. Do the arguments answer the specific questions you ask?

Step 8. Revise your analysis. After discussing your analysis with your classmates and friends, you will want to respond to their comments by doing additional research or presenting a more balanced view. Remember that at this point you are a neutral observer and will avoid committing yourself. This revised analysis will form the basis of the rest of your work on this project. Here is an example of a completed issue analysis.

1

SHOULD JUDGES HAVE THE POWER TO COMMIT THE MENTALLY ILL TO INSTITUTIONS AGAINST THEIR WILL?

by Patti Cohen

CONTEXT.

Throughout history there have been various ways of dealing with the mentally ill, from shipping them away to killing them with poisonous drugs. However, in 1773 the first institution solely for the mentally ill was established in Williamsburg and the debate over proper commitment laws began.

In 1845 the Massachusetts Supreme Court ruled that an individual could be involuntarily committed to a mental institution if he or she was "dangerous to himself or others" and it was this decision which served as a foundation for most state statutes.

The process which leads up to the actual commitment is fairly simple. Anyone from a friend to a parent is able to petition for the possible institutionalization of another. From there an examining committee hands down their report to the judge, who makes the final decision.

ISSUES AND ARGUMENTS

2

LIST OF PRO ARGUMENTS.

1. Involuntary commitment is necessary in order to
    provide treatment to those who need profes-
    sional help.
2. Involuntary commitment is crucial in order to
    prevent the mentally ill from attempting
    suicide.
3. Society must have some means for controlling
    those who would be harmful to society. Involun-
    tary civil commitment is a mechanism by which
    society can protect itself against possible
    violence.

WHO MAKES THESE ARGUMENTS AND WHY?

1. The first argument is made by George Griffith,
    the senior judge of Fairfax County, Virginia,
    and other judges. Their intentions are sincere
    and for the good of the mentally ill person.
2. The second argument is made by Dr. Paul Mar-
    delle and other psychiatrists. Their reasons
    for supporting involuntary commitment are also
    in the interest of the ill person. Dr. Mardelle

70

3

has dealt with many suicides and believes that civil commitment saves lives.

3. Seymour Halleck, a psychiatrist, makes this argument. He is concerned with the safety of society.

SPECIFIC ACTIONS THE PROS SHOULD TAKE.

Since involuntary hospitalization is legal in all states, the proponents of civil commitment are not in the same position as the opponents. Action on the part of the supporters is not as necessary since what they advocate is already being carried out. To make civil commitment even more defensible, proponents should:

1. Persuade the states to spend more money on their mental institutions. By improving the facilities and staff, more patients will be "cured" and conditions will be less subject to criticism.

2. Urge legislators to make civil commitment proceedings as fair as possible, including adequate psychiatric examinations.

4

LIST OF CON ARGUMENTS.

1. Involuntary commitment is punishment without
   trial, imprisonment without time limit, and
   stigmatization without the hope of redress.
2. Being potentially dangerous is not a crime, and
   psychiatrists cannot predict violent behavior.
3. Involuntary commitment violates the Fifth
   Amendment right to refusal on grounds of self-
   incrimination by forcing one to be interviewed
   by a psychiatrist.
4. Involuntary confinement for "mental illness" is
   a deprivation of liberty, which violates basic
   human rights guaranteed by the U.S.
   Constitution.
5. Mental institutions are not giving the so-
   called mentally ill appropriate treatment once
   involuntarily institutionalized.
6. The process of involuntary commitment is
   arbitrary.

WHO MAKES THESE ARGUMENTS AND WHY?

1. The first four arguments are made by Thomas
   Szaz, a leading opponent of civil commitment.

5

Szaz and other members of the American Civil
Liberties Union are deeply concerned with individual rights and the deprivation of personal
liberty. Szaz and the ACLU feel involuntary
civil commitment violates the Bill of Rights.

2. Tom Donaldson makes the fifth argument. Donaldson was an actual victim of involuntary commitment. He was institutionalized in a Florida
State Hospital for fifteen years. He is seeking
to spare others the cruelty he suffered.

3. Kent Miller, a prominent clinical researcher,
makes argument six. He believes that there is
too much variation from judge to judge and jurisdiction to jurisdiction in the way individuals with similar "symptoms" are treated.

SPECIFIC ACTIONS THE CONS SHOULD TAKE.

Opponents should try to persuade legislators:

1. To treat civil commitment cases as we do criminal cases. The allegedly dangerous mentally ill
should enjoy the same rights of notice and
hearing, appointment of an attorney and jury
trial that a criminal defendant enjoys.

6

2. To require proof of violent, criminal actions. Involuntary commitment should not be permitted merely on the grounds that an individual is mentally ill.

3. To implement a process of periodic review of each committed person's progress. Patients must be able to petition the courts for release at any time.

4. To require that judges who preside over commitment proceedings be trained in mental illness.

REFERENCES.

Bean, P. (1980). Compulsory admission to mental hospitals. New York: Wiley. (Context)

Boodman, S. (1984, January 8). The world of involuntary commitment. The Washington Post, pp. 1, 11. (Con)

Halleck, S. (1969, March). The reform of mental hospitals. Psychology Today, 2, 39. (Pro)

Miller, K. (1976). Managing madness: The case against civil commitment. New York: Macmillan. (Con)

7

Szaz, T. (1969, March). The crime of commitment.

Psychology Today, 2, 55. (Con)

_____(1981). Psychiatric slavery. New York: Free

Press. (Con)

Warren, C. A. B. (1982). The court of last resort:

mental illness and the law. Chicago: University

of Chicago Press. (Context)

Wexler, D. (1981). Mental health laws. New York:

Plenum Press. (Context)

THIRD STAGE: TAKING A STAND ON AN ISSUE

Step 9. After weighing the evidence, which side of the issue do you find more convincing? Which side will you advocate? Explore these questions by writing freely for ten minutes or so. During the ten-minute "free write" many students "rehearse" the arguments they will make, though not in great detail. Part of this rehearsal often includes some treatment of the opposition, which is called for in the final essay. The following discovery writing, in which the author refers to her issue analysis, is an example:

```
    "Should the Diablo Canyon nuclear power plant
be permitted to go on line?" The opponents of Dia-
blo Canyon have a more persuasive argument than the
proponents. The first point on plant safety is a
legitimate concern; even if the plant has been
strengthened, is it enough?
    The arguments about citizen participation are
probably the most compelling. Any decision that
could have such a major effect on people should
leave room for their input in making the decision.
The procedural arguments about starting the plant
before public hearings are completed is important
because people can be excluded from making other
decisions as well.
    The antinuclear arguments are compelling, but
hard to prove. The utilities can find as much in-
formation supporting nuclear power as antinuclear
groups can find against it. Safety arguments are
legitimate, but based mostly on "what ifs."
                        -- Nancy Wonkka
```

What is particularly interesting about this piece of informal writing is that the author lists the major arguments supporting her position, opposition to the licensing of Diablo Canyon, but immediately weighs them against the refutations of the proponents of licensing and expresses doubt about the adequacy of her initial opinion. The expressive writing reveals the tension of the internal dialogue taking place. Not surprisingly, Nancy reversed herself and argued in the final draft in behalf of licensing the controversial power plant. Early in the finished paper, she says, alluding to herself:

```
Many of the reasons why people oppose nuclear power
stem from the fact that they do not understand it.
```

76

```
It is a highly technical and complex field; people
feel intimidated. Opposing it is easier than trying
to learn about nuclear power.
```

Many students will change their initial opinions on their issue. The continual researching, drafting, and revising stimulate reflection.

Step 10. Write a draft of your argument, employing the following structure:

    introduction and context

    thesis and presentation of evidence

    refutation of other side

    conclusion

The draft is the second major writing exercise. You will write the draft from the issue analysis. You will find this term paper significantly easier to write than papers in other courses where you did not follow a sequence of prewriting steps. The context section of the issue analysis will be the basis of part one of the draft, introduction and context. Your list of pro and con arguments will provide the material for parts two, thesis and presentation of evidence, and three, refutation of other side. In the conclusion you will state clearly the specific action you are striving to persuade the reader to take. The references will provide a bibliography for the term paper.

Step 11. Distribute copies of your draft to others and ask them to indicate parts that are especially effective and places where they want more information. Your fellow students can provide valuable feedback that you can incorporate into the revision. Here are two excerpts from responses of students who read their drafts aloud to two other students and received comments:

```
The members of the group had some good criticism
and also brought up some good points on the other
side of the issue.
                            -- David Powers
```

```
Reading my paper out loud helped me in the respect
that I could feel where it was weak and my argument
was choppy.
                            -- Lesley Kachadorian
```

Step 12. Revise and edit your draft. You will find that your revised term paper is significantly better than the rough draft. At this point, pay attention to organization, logic, syntax, grammar, diction, spelling, and punctuation. (See Chapters 9 and 10.) Your final paper should be clear, concise, and coherent.

Step 13. Type your paper (or have it typed). A suggested length is five to eight double-spaced pages. A good idea is to proofread the typescript yourself and ask one or two others to read it for errors as well.

Issues and Arguments: Steps to a Successful Analysis

I. Choosing an Issue

Step 1. Write a list of four or five controversial issues related to your course.

Step 2. Share and discuss your list with others.

Step 3. Choose one issue and write freely for five minutes about what you know and don't know about the issue.

Step 4. Frame your issue as a question (e.g., Should handguns be banned?)

II. Analyzing an Issue

Step 5. Research the issue you've chosen.

Step 6. Write a balanced analysis, but do not take a position. Your analysis should have the following headings:

issue (in the form of a question)

context (background a reader needs in order to understand the arguments)

pro arguments (list and number)

who makes these arguments and why

some specific actions the pros should take (list)

con arguments (list and number)

who makes these arguments and why

some specific actions the cons should take (list)

references (identify as pro, con, or context)

Step 7. Show your analysis to others.

Step 8. Revise your analysis.

III. *Taking a Stand on an Issue*

Your argument will take the form of a well-organized, five- to eight-page essay.

> Step 9. After weighing the evidence, which side of the issue do you find more convincing? Which side will you advocate? Explore these questions by writing freely for ten minutes or so.

> Step 10. Write a draft of your argument, employing the following structure:
> > introduction and context
> > thesis and presentation of evidence
> > refutation of other side
> > conclusion

> Step 11. Distribute copies of your draft to others and ask them to indicate parts that are especially effective and places where they want more information.

> Step 12. Revise and edit your draft.

> Step 13. Give typed essay to your instructor.

[5] *Policy Analysis*

The philosophers have only *interpreted* the world, in various ways; the point, however, is to *change* it.

—Karl Marx

When President Richard Nixon appointed a new Undersecretary at the Department of Labor in 1971, the President wanted to see some changes made. Shortly after taking his new post, former banker Laurence H. Silberman asked a simple question: "Tell me," he inquired of senior officials in the Manpower Administration, "which of your programs most successfully prepare the chronically unemployed for the labor market?" Although these officials had almost ten years of experience in designing and administering such programs and had spent billions of dollars, they had no answer. In fact, they regarded the question as a threat to their own job security. After that, Mr. Silberman built a group of hard-nosed evaluators to

81

answer such questions. He discovered that generally the best evaluators were social scientists trained in policy analysis, brought into
government temporarily from the universities. As a result of their
work, several existing programs were scrapped or modified and
new, more effective programs created.

Government decision makers increasingly rely on this new
breed of social scientists, called policy analysts, to provide answers
to tough questions. Policy analysts are more concerned with influencing political behavior than in explaining or predicting it. For
them, knowledge is no longer an end in itself. Instead it becomes a
means to bring about a better world. Policy analysis, in fact, is the
fastest-growing subfield in political science.

Policy analysis is an approach for measuring the costs and benefits of alternative solutions to a social problem and for selecting
the best course of action. Its techniques can also be used to evaluate
the success of existing government programs.

A policy is a general rule, designed to influence the behavior
and circumstances of large numbers of people now and in the future. Some of society's most important decisions take the form of
government policies and reflect that society's values and resources.
Policy analysis differs from *issue* analysis in that there are usually
more than two policy options from which to choose. Policy analysis
involves six steps:

1. recognition of a social problem
2. identification of objectives to be achieved in its solution
3. deciding what alternative solutions are available
4. judging how the alternatives relate to the objectives
5. weighting the objectives
6. choosing the best alternative.

In the following pages we will look at each of these steps in turn.
By doing each assignment, you will write a policy analysis.

Step 1: Recognize a Problem

The policy analyst begins with a problem. You can identify social
problems by reading newspapers, news magazines, and scholarly
journals or simply by observing your surroundings.

> If you walk the streets of an inner city, you will probably notice
> many signs of decay — burned-out abandoned buildings, gar-

bage-strewn vacant lots. Obviously, many former residents of the neighborhood have moved elsewhere, probably to the suburbs. Who can deny that urban blight is a social problem of great magnitude and importance? Reading the newspaper you may notice that the costs of medical care are rising at a far more rapid pace than inflation. Can someone without health insurance afford medical services at today's prices? The rising cost of health care is another significant social problem.

Problems, then, are all around us. We have selected one to use as an initial example in our explanation of how to conduct policy analysis: white-collar crime. An additional example we will refer to concerns plea bargaining.

WRITING 5.1: IDENTIFYING SOCIAL PROBLEMS. On the basis of your reading or observation, select three social problems. Unless your professor requests a more formal treatment, discuss them in your journal. This writing is the first of a series that will lead you toward the completion of a policy analysis. Don't look for solutions in your statement of the problem; that comes later. Do try to summarize the observations which led you to conclude certain phenomena constitute "problems" for society. For example, here's how Jennie described the white-collar-crime problem:

```
White-collar crime, such as padding expense ac-
counts, means higher prices for all of us con-
sumers. But so often it goes unpunished. Unlike the
poor teenage mugger who gets sent away for years,
Mr. Big Shot swindler gets off free. It's not fair!
It's also getting so that my parents don't know if
they should trust their stock broker! One more
thing that hit me is that if the big boys cheat on
income taxes, why shouldn't we all? And they want
me to pay back student loans someday? Ha!
```

Step 2: Identify the Objectives to Be Achieved by the Solution

What objectives should the solution bring about? In order to draw up a list of objectives you will need to do some reading about the general problem. Advocates and opponents of specific reforms may only imply what the appropriate goals for the policy maker should be without stating them explicitly or precisely. You, the policy analyst, however, can't afford fuzzy thinking.

The White-Collar-Crime Problem

Social scientists distinguish white-collar crime from street crime, such as murder, rape, and burglary, and from organized crime, such as prostitution, loan sharking, and drug dealing. White-collar criminals tend to come from the middle class. The four broad categories of this crime are (1) frauds against government, e.g., tax evasion and political corruption; (2) frauds against consumers, e.g., sale of worthless securities; (3) frauds against business, e.g., embezzlement and pilferage; and (4) corporate illegality, e.g., antitrust violations and environmental offenses.

The policy analyst might decide that any strategy selected to combat white-collar crime should achieve the following objectives: (1) reduce the incidence of crime; (2) be affordable; (3) avoid interfering with legitimate activities; (4) be politically feasible, that is, have a realistic chance of being adopted; and (5) support the moral values of society.

PERSONAL WRITING 5.A. Policy analysis is applicable whenever one needs to decide among a number of alternatives and wherever several objectives need to be fulfilled. The process works for personal problem solving and for business decision making as well as for public sector choices. To see how this works, use your journal to begin a series of personal writings. List four or five objectives for your future career (perhaps such goals as a specific geographic location, security, variety of challenges, high income, public service, working with people). Alternative: List four or five major goals of your college education. Later you'll have a chance to analyze your list.

WRITING 5.2: IDENTIFYING OBJECTIVES. Select one of the three social problems you identified in Writing 5.1. On the basis of reading and observation define the problem as sharply as possible, breaking it into subproblems as needed. Then draw up a list of four or five objectives that the ideal solution would achieve.

Step 3: Identify Alternative Solutions

For most problems, reformers will put forward a variety of possible solutions. One of them, or a certain combination of two or more of them, will be the optimal program, the alternative that best satisfies the objectives. One possible alternative for any problem is to do nothing, that is, preserve the status quo. You can identify possible solutions by reading about the problem you are trying to solve.

Now let's consider some alternative solutions to the problem of white-collar crime. Four major approaches are discussed most often: rehabilitation, punishment, regulation, and *laissez-faire*. Based on the assumption that criminal attitudes are learned, some sociologists suggest that crime can be reduced by making it morally unthinkable. They advocate programs that would rehabilitate the white-collar offender, i.e., change his or her attitudes and values.

The punitive approach assumes that criminal behavior is the result of rational weighing of the relative costs and benefits of criminal versus noncriminal behavior. The solution, then, is to increase the costs of crime either by increasing the severity of punishment or by increasing the chances of apprehension, for example, through greater use of "sting" operations. The punitive model stresses deterrence and retribution rather than rehabilitation.

The regulatory strategy relies on the manipulation of incentives, stressing rewards such as tax breaks or subsidies and government contracts to law-abiding corporations.

Advocates of the *laissez-faire* strategy believe that competition in the marketplace can significantly reduce the amount of socially undesirable behavior. According to this view, consumers who buy defective products can simply stop patronizing the offending producer or seller and buy from others. This solution would require the decriminalization of much of the behavior now classified as white-collar crime.

PERSONAL WRITING 5.B.   List in your journal four or five different specific careers (such as lawyer in corporate practice, military officer, hotel management) that you think might satisfy some or all of the objectives you listed in Personal Writing 5.A — in other words, list alternative solutions. Add a few sentences telling what it is about each that might be appropriate for you.

> WRITING 5.3: Identify four or five alternative solutions to the social problem you chose in Writing 5.2. Remember that doing nothing is always a choice.

Step 4: Determine How the Alternatives Relate to the Objective

The policy analyst next determines how well each alternative solution relates to each of the listed objectives. The question you will ask is whether a given alternative achieves a particular goal. Let's compare the punitive and *laissez-faire* strategies for reducing white-collar crime and add the other policy options later. Usually the simplest way of summarizing your results will be in the form of a table such as the one shown below:

Table 1. *Objectives, Alternatives, and Relations in Containing White-Collar Crime*

	Alternative Strategies	
Objectives	Punitive	Laissez-Faire
1. White-collar crime reduction	−	−
2. Inexpensiveness	−	+
3. Avoidance of interference with legitimate business activities	−	+
4. Political feasibility	+	−
5. Support for morality	+	−
Unweighted sum of pluses	2	2

Explanation of the Table. In Table 1 (based on Holland 1983), a " + " means that the alternative satisfies that particular objective. A " − " indicates that it doesn't. Let's look at the punitive strategy first, as shown in the first vertical + / − column. The historical expansion of criminal liability is evidence of the political popularity of punishment as a solution to social problems. We can thus place a " + " in the column beside "political feasibility." Legislatures are especially attracted to punishment when offenses are considered immoral. Criminal penalties express the community's moral outrage at fraud and corruption and reinforce its principles of acceptable conduct. Thus, we place a " + " beside "support for morality."

The costs of criminalizing immorality and harnessing the criminal justice system to regulate more and more socially undesirable behavior are substantial. Each addition to the penal law must be matched by an extra commitment of law enforcement resources. Efficient enforcement of the tax and kickback laws would result in the conviction of millions of people each year, creating demands for more courts and prisons. We thus place a " − " beside the criterion of "inexpensiveness." Experience demonstrates that enforcers prefer civil and administrative measures to criminal prosecutions of white-collar criminals and that judges continue to dispense lenient sentences, such as probation. We therefore place a " − " next to "crime reduction."

Criminalization and full enforcement might seriously interfere with legitimate business activity. Because it is often hard to distinguish illegal activity from aggressive-but-legal business activity, strict enforcement would have a cooling effect on certain legitimate transactions. Extra record-keeping requirements to aid detection, for example, are a costly burden on businesses. We therefore put a " − " next to "avoidance of interference."

Now let us relate the *laissez-faire* strategy to the goals. A policy of decriminalization and deregulation involves removing government from the scene. This means that of the four proposed strategies, the *laissez-faire* alternative is cheapest and interferes the least with economic activities. Accordingly, we put a " + " next to objectives 2 and 3 in Table 1.

A major objection to *laissez-faire* is that legislators would not accept it. Some opinion surveys show widespread public support for criminal proceedings, especially in cases involving governmental corruption and environmental damage. A " − " is thus appropriate next to goal 4. Another weakness is that whenever society decriminalizes an activity, it implicitly condones it. We therefore place a " − " beside criterion 5. Finally, although decriminalization will reduce the amount of measured crime, it will not significantly reduce the behavior itself. We accordingly put a " − " next to goal 1 as well.

Now we're ready to add the number of pluses under each strategy. The sum for the punitive approach is 2, the same as that for the *laissez-faire* strategy. At this point in the analysis, the two very different solutions seem to achieve the objectives equally well (or equally poorly).

> PERSONAL WRITING 5.C.   Relate each of the possible career choices to each of the objectives you identified in Personal Writing 5.A (or relate possible majors to each of the goals you identified for a college education). Draw up a table relating alternatives to objectives. Be sure to total the pluses in each column.

> WRITING 5.4:   Compose a table relating the alternative solutions you identified in Writing 5.3 to the attributes of the best solution you listed in Writing 5.2. Compute the sum of the pluses and include the results in your table.

Step 5: Weight the Objectives

Not all the criteria for a good policy will be of equal importance. As you consider each objective you must determine its relative value and assign a weight to it. The simplest weighting scheme is "more" or "less" important. The more important objectives receive a weight of 2, and the less important a weight of 1.

With regard to our white-collar-crime example, there is no agreement among analysts on the comparative weight to be assigned to the five objectives, but let's make some assumptions. Table 2 is based on the premise that actually shrinking the incidence of criminality while avoiding the social harm of interfering with the market place is more important than reducing expense, respecting political reality, and reinforcing communal values. This weighting scheme obviously stresses individual autonomy and economic freedom and may not coincide with your values. It is unlikely that any two analysts will agree perfectly on weights to be given to the criteria, but each must be able to justify the assumptions giving rise to the weighting used.

Table 2. *Efforts to Contain White-Collar Crime*

Objectives	Weights
1. White-collar crime reduction	more (2)
2. Inexpensiveness	less (1)
3. Avoidance of interference with legitimate business activities	more (2)
4. Political feasibility	less (1)
5. Support for morality	less (1)

More precise weighting can be achieved by replacing "more"/ "less" with a rank ordering from 5 to 1. Instead of scoring each solution more (2) or less (1) for each goal (the binary method), the 5, 4, 3, 2, 1 system allows middling scores. The more specific the level of analysis, the more precise the comparative weighting can be. For example, if we were talking about specific kinds of white-collar crimes such as antitrust violations or defrauding the government, instead of white-collar crime in general, the scoring would probably change.

> PERSONAL WRITING 5.D.   Assign weights to the career objectives (or goals of a sound college education) you worked on in your journal for Personal Writing 5.A. Use either the binary (2/1) or the rank-order (5,4,3,2,1) method. Justify your weighting scheme.

> WRITING 5.5: WEIGHTING THE OBJECTIVES.   Assign weights, using either the binary or rank-ordering scheme, to the objectives of a sound policy solution identified in Writing 5.2. Justify your assignment of weights. On what assumptions is it based?

Step 6: Choose the Best Alternative

In the preceding steps, you determined the likely costs and benefits expected from each policy option. You, the analyst, did this to reduce uncertainties about possible choices. Now you are ready to select the optimum program, the one that maximizes achievement of your stated goals.

First you must convert the pluses and minuses in Table 1 into numbers. Each plus (+) means that the strategy achieves that objective, and each minus (−) means that it does not, at least compared to other strategies. For example, the *laissez-faire* strategy *is* inexpensive (objective #2), but the punitive strategy, relatively speaking, is not. Score each plus as 2 and each minus as 1. Then multiply each of these numbers (relation scores) by the weights (more = 2 and less = 1) assigned to each objective. Because the regulatory strategy does reduce white-collar crime and because crime reduction is weighted as important, the resulting product is +2 × 2, or +4. After multiplying the relation scores by the weights for each objective and each strategy, total the products. This process is illustrated in Table 3.

You should ignore the pluses and minuses when summing the

Table 3. *Objectives, Alternatives, Relations, Weights, and Choices in Containing White-Collar Crime*

| Objectives | Weights | Alternative Strategies | | | |
		Rehabili-tative	Punitive	Regula-tory	Laissez-faire
1. Reduce crime	more (2)	−(2)	−(2)	+(4)	−(2)
2. Inexpensive	less (1)	−(1)	−(1)	−(1)	+(2)
3. Non-interference with more business	more (2)	−(2)	−(2)	+(4)	+(4)
4. Feasibility	less (1)	−(1)	+(2)	+(2)	−(1)
5. Moral support	less (1)	+(2)	+(2)	−(1)	−(1)
Unweighted sum of pluses		1	2	3	2
Weighted sum of pluses		8	9	12	10

products. Notice that, according to the unweighted sum of the pluses, the punitive and *laissez-faire* strategies are equally good. However, when we take into account the goal weights, *laissez-faire* exceeds punitive by 10 to 9. Notice also that a policy stressing rewards, the regulatory strategy, exceeds the others both in terms of the unweighted sum of the pluses (3) and the weighted sum of the products (12).

> PERSONAL WRITING 5.E. Construct a table comparing possible ideal careers (or majors). Is there a difference in which choice is best when you take into account the weight you assigned to the objectives you identified in Personal Writing 5.D?

> WRITING 5.6: CHOOSING THE BEST ALTERNATIVE. Construct a table comparing possible solutions to your selected social problem. When you factor the weight scores into the calculations, does the preferred policy change?

PART/WHOLE PERCENTAGING

One of the shortcomings of the method we have used for comparing policy options is that it can tell us which is the best *single* policy and produce the ranking of the alternatives, but it cannot identify the optimum *mix* of solutions, as we confront a number of problems simultaneously. Nor does it allow us to allocate a budget among policy alternatives. Part/whole percentaging analysis is a simple way of doing just this. This kind of analysis involves converting the raw scores of each alternative policy on each objective into a part/whole percentage. We do this by adding up the raw scores for each objective and dividing each raw score by the total. After assigning relative weights to each objective, we can total up the part/whole percentages across the objectives for each policy option. We must identify those objectives we wish to minimize and those we wish to maximize. We subtract part/whole percentages for the former and add them for the latter. Confused? Let's make things more concrete by examining another policy problem, plea bargaining.

The Problem of Plea Bargaining

Plea bargaining is the practice of negotiation between the state and the criminally accused, whereby the defendant pleads guilty in exchange for a reduction in the charge or the sentence. Some people believe that the lack of trials due to plea bargaining is a serious social problem. Others defend a system in which 90% of the defendants successfully negotiate a plea. To decide whether the criminal justice system should emphasize trials or plea bargains, we must identify the appropriate goals or attributes of the best method of disposing of criminal cases. Two very important criteria are (1) how much time the method consumes, and (2) whether and to what degree it generates respect for the law.

Taking the two primary alternatives for processing cases — the trial versus the plea bargain approach — we can follow the previously outlined steps to determine which is better, given our goals of limited time consumption and respect for law. Let's go beyond the either/or kind of conclusion, however, and consider the possibility of a policy mix. This extra step is more realistic, as, for example, a common question would be that of how to allocate the criminal justice budget among different programs. What percentage of the budget should go for the funding of trials, and what percentage should go to fund plea bargaining? In other words, what is the optimum combination of trials and bargained guilty pleas?

The first task is to determine the relative weights of each objective. Let's say that our reading leads us to determine that inculcating respect for the judicial process, the legitimacy of the courts, is three times as important as speed in the processing of the criminally accused. Remember, you must always be prepared to justify your weighting of the goals; in a finished policy analysis, you would provide documentation. Secondly, we must develop raw scores for each of our criteria: time and respect. Under the dimension of time, we know from the literature that the average time from arrest to disposition where the defendant is tried is 120 days, and where the defendant pleads guilty in exchange for concessions from the prosecutor the time consumed is 30 days. We now total these raw scores: $120 + 30 = 150$. Since 150 days represents the total, trials must account for 80% of total time consumed and pleas 20%. We wish to minimize time consumption, so we place a minus sign ($-$) before each of these percentages. See Table 4 on page 94 (based on Nagel 1984).

The extent to which an alternative promotes respect for law is more difficult to quantify. It cannot be measured in days or dollars, so we must construct a scale that indicates the degree to which one policy increases respect relative to others. The easiest such scales to use run from 0 to 10. A reading of the literature suggests that disposition by trial measurably increases respect for the court system (Kipnis 1976). Therefore, let's assign a score of 6 to disposition by trial and only 2 to disposition by plea bargaining. We total these raw scores and calculate that 6 represents 75% of the total (6/8), and 2 represents 25% of the total (2/8). Wishing to maximize respect for the courts, we treat these percentages as positive rather than negative numbers.

The object of policy analysis is to choose the alternative that will provide the greatest benefits minus the costs, i.e., that will have the best cost/benefit ratio. In order to choose the best policy option, we multiply the weight assigned to each objective by the part/whole percent. Because "respect for law" has a weight of 3, we multiply $3 \times +75\%$ for trials and $3 \times +25\%$ for pleas. We do the same for time consumption, which is very easy because it has a weight of one. We then add the weighted scores for each alternative:

Trials: $(1 \times -80\%) + (3 \times +75\%) = +145\%$
Pleas: $(1 \times -20\%) + (3 \times +25\%) = +55\%$

Thus trials yield 145 relative units in benefits minus costs, while pleas yield 55 relative units in benefits minus costs. Therefore, if we must choose one alternative, we choose trials as the more profitable approach. If you are working with only two alternatives, the unweighted sums will always be the same, although with opposite signs. The difference in sign is irrelevant for this particular calculation.

The part/whole percentaging technique allows us to do more than select the best alternative; it permits us to allocate resources in the optimal way across all alternatives. We simply take the weighted sums and convert them to percentages that equal 100%.

Table 4. *Comparing Alternative Means For Disposing of Criminal Prosecutions*

| | Objectives | | | | Overall Scores | | |
| | Time Consumption (Weight = 1) | | Respect for Law (Weight = 3) | | For Choosing | | For Allocating |
Alternatives	Raw Score (Days)	Part/Whole Percent	Raw Score (0–10)	Part/Whole Percent	Unweighted Sum	Weighted Sum	Part/Whole Percent
Trials	120	−80%	6	+75%	−5%	+145%	+72.5%
Pleas	30	−20%	2	+25%	+5%	+55%	+27.5%
Totals	150	100%	8	100%	0%	200%	100%

Because we must divide the weighted sum total (200%) by 2 to obtain 100%, we must also divide each of the weighted sums (145% and 55%) by 2. The optimum allocation of the criminal justice budget or optimum allocation of prosecutorial effort, therefore, is 72.5% to disposition by trials and 27.5% to disposition by negotiated pleas, approximately the reverse of the existing allocation!

PERSONAL WRITING 5.F. How could this discussion of part/whole percentaging possibly apply to your journal writings on choosing a career (or major) and maximizing your gains from college attendance? If you don't see an immediate relationship, try rephrasing the "goals" of Personal Writing 5.A. The problem then in part becomes one of allocating your resources, including time and money, to accomplishing several objectives with a mix of strategies.

WRITING THE POLICY ANALYSIS

For most policy analysts, doing the tables and calculations using either the standard method or part/whole percentaging is only part of the job. To affect decision making you must also communicate the results. For this you compose the true policy analysis.

The first considerations are audience and purpose, as discussed in Chapter 1. You are writing the analysis for a policy maker, such as a legislator or administrator. Your goal is to persuade that person or group to select the option or combination of options that will solve a social problem to the maximum extent possible, generating the greatest benefits at the least cost. The tone of your summary should be objective. There are similarities between the policy analysis and the empirical research report in that you must do your best to exclude your personal biases or values from the analysis. The weights you assign to various objectives, for example, generally must come from the priorities of the legislator or other person(s) who must use the final analysis. These weights may reflect the narrow views of a special interest group or the broad views of the general constituency back home. In a paper for classroom use, you will be assigning weights based on your own preferences and these must be clearly explained and identified. Similarly, a table, although critical, cannot speak for itself. You must carefully explain how you arrived at each of the numbers and signs that appear. Also, you must be especially clear when you define your assumptions — these generally belong right in the beginning of your essay — and explain your results.

WRITING 5.7: WRITING THE POLICY ANALYSIS. Using the table you designed in Writing 5.6, write a policy analysis of 10 to 20 pages. The following summary outlines the steps.

Steps in Policy Analysis

1. Define the social problem. Provide background the reader needs to appreciate the debate over what to do about it.
2. Identify the objectives to be achieved by the ideal solution. Give the sources of these criteria.
3. Identify the alternative policies that have been proposed as solutions to the problem. Tell what is distinct about each program or approach.
4. Explain how each alternative relates to each objective. Would it increase or decrease the amount of each objective? Can you estimate the degree to which it increases or decreases that amount? Consider the alternatives as independent variables and the objectives as dependent variables. A variance in the former will produce a variance in the latter.
5. Weight the objectives. Explain the importance of each criterion. State the facts and assumptions on which the weighting is based.
6. Select the best alternative or combination of alternatives. Explain why one policy or subset of policies is the optimum choice.
7. Conclude with a list of references cited (see Chapter 8).

| 6 | The Research Proposal and Research Report

PREVIEW: *Designing and conducting empirical research is the path to understanding human behavior followed by many political scientists. This chapter explains how to present in writing the fruits of such research.*

The fact/value distinction and the scientific study of politics
The research proposal
The research report

FACT: The national crime rate was lower in 1985 than in preceding years.

What explains this fact? President Reagan and Attorney General Meese were quick to take the credit. They attributed the fall in crime to more efficient police work and tougher sentencing by judges — goals consistently advocated and supported by the administration. Several political scientists and criminologists, however, cried "Nonsense!" They pointed out that, according to empirical data, the drop in crime rates is almost completely explained by the declining percentage of eighteen-year-olds in the population.

THE FACT/VALUE DISTINCTION AND THE SCIENTIFIC STUDY OF POLITICS

Questions of this sort — why people behave as they do — capture the interest of many students of politics. Known as behavioralists, these men and women use the scientific method to understand political behavior. Distinguishing between facts and values, they seek to explain why political actors do what they do, not to show how people ought to act. In other words, they emphasize what *is,* not what *ought to be.*

The behavioralist approach to the study of political science is empirical, that is, it relies on observation rather than speculation. Empirical statements refer to the world of sensory experience and can therefore be verified — proven true or false. The assertion "Republicans tend to be wealthier than Democrats" is an empirical statement that is either true or false. Behavioralists shun normative statements such as "Democracy is a better form of government than monarchy" and "Freedom is of greater worth than equality" because no amount of empirical evidence can prove or disprove them.

Research is inspired by wonder, the beginning of wisdom in learning from the world. The empirical researcher begins with a question about the world and then designs a study to answer that question. "Why are some countries more stable than others?" "What determines whether a nation is more likely to resolve conflicts with its neighbors by war or by peaceful means?" "What kinds of citizens are least likely to vote in presidential elections in the United States?" The goal is to explain or predict political phenomena by applying the scientific method, which you may recall from your study of biology or chemistry. This method of inquiry consists of five steps:

1. defining a problem
2. collecting data
3. summarizing the data
4. explaining the data
5. deducing hypotheses for further testing.

This chapter is not an essay on how to apply the scientific method, though. Your instructor will teach you the principles of research or will refer you to a good book on methodology.

The purpose of this chapter is to help you write two documents: *the research proposal,* which precedes the actual research, and *the research report.* Given the limitations of time and resources, your instructor may ask you to draw up a proposal that is logically sound and feasible but not require that you actually carry it out.

THE RESEARCH PROPOSAL

In the research proposal you are engaged in Step 1 of the scientific method — defining a problem. The process of defining a problem also consists of five steps: (1) choosing a general topic, (2) reviewing previous studies, (3) stating the hypothesis, (4) operationalizing the concepts, and (5) developing a strategy for testing the hypothesis. Your goal is to propose a research design that if carried out would answer the question you pose about the world.

Step 1: Choose a Topic

We have discussed how to choose a topic in Chapter 4 (Issues and Arguments) and Chapter 5 (Policy Analysis), and we discuss it again in Chapter 7 (Principles of Research and Basic Bibliographies). Most of what is said elsewhere applies to selecting a topic for empirical study. Two rules, however, are particularly important in this kind of research: The topic must not be overly broad, and it must pose a problem that is solvable. The narrowing of the topic is the most important step in research.

Just how do you find a topic? Perhaps while reading your textbook or reviewing class notes you notice that a much higher percentage of middle-class citizens voted in the 1984 presidential election than lower-class citizens. This fact puzzles you and you wonder if this was true in previous elections. If income is consistently associated with the percentage of eligible voters who turn out at the polls, what explains this phenomenon? You will want your explanation to be simple, to have important implications, and to enable you to make predictions about political behavior. Given a person's annual income, can you predict accurately what the chances are of that person voting in a particular election? In a democracy it is obviously important to know the conditions that must be present if citizens are going to participate in the political process. The relationship between income and voter turnout is, thus, a good topic for investigation.

WRITING 6.1: CHOOSING A PROBLEM. Every treatment of a political subject contains both the author's opinions and assertions of fact. For example, the author of an article on capital punishment might express the opinion that capital punishment should be abolished based in part upon the "fact" that executions do not deter murder. As a reader you might wonder whether this assertion is true. Your task would be to determine the truth by empirical testing. You are not concerned with opinions because they cannot be verified by the scientific method. For the first step of writing a research proposal, select a general topic (like capital punishment or nuclear deterrence), then read an article on that topic. List three opinions expressed by the author and three facts. One of these facts will form the basis of your research proposal.

Step 2: Review Previous Studies

Now that you have isolated a problem, i.e., an interesting fact in need of an explanation, the next step is to find out what is already known about it. What if you discover that your topic has been thoroughly researched, that explanations of the phenomenon in question are well established? Then you may wish to look for a field where researchers have done fewer studies or where there is less confidence in the theoretical explanation. A respectable kind of research, however, is replication, which in fact forms a major portion of the scientific study of politics. Replication is the repetition of an experiment to reduce the probability of error. Each time researchers repeat a particular study and produce identical results, they increase our confidence in the validity of the original finding.

If little or no work has been done on a topic, beware: This might be an indication that the problem is relatively insignificant, that little variance exists among the cases for you to explain, or that the relevant data may be unattainable. The lack of published research, however, may also be a sign that you have selected an area of fruitful research.

As you read the scholarly literature, ask what hypotheses the authors were testing, what the relevant concepts are and how they defined them, what methodological procedures they used for testing the hypotheses, and what their research design was. Science is a cumulative enterprise. Take good notes as you read, then, because you will wish to incorporate the findings and theories of your predecessors. As you read you may also find yourself modifying your original problem. In fact, you may frame and discard several statements of what puzzles you.

> WRITING 6.2: COMPILING A WORKING BIBLIOG-RAPHY. Develop a ten-item bibliography for one of the facts, or problems, you selected in the previous exercise. Include both books and articles. For each citation, provide a one-sentence summary of the material. For assistance in locating reports of past research, see Chapter 7, "Principles of Research and Basic Bibliographies."

Step 3: State the Hypothesis

We concluded step 1 with a question: Why do members of the upper and middle socioeconomic classes vote in higher percentages than members of the working and lower classes? Now we must transform the question into a hypothesis so we can test whether a certain kind of relationship exists between the two facts. We are attempting to explain why something does or doesn't occur. We must phrase our hypothesis in a positive manner, as a declarative sentence, not as a question — not "As citizens' income increases, does the likelihood of their voting increase?" but "As citizens' income increases, their likelihood of going to the polls increases."

A hypothesis is a supposition formulated from observed facts and presented as a temporary explanation in order to establish a basis for research. Hypotheses are "if/then" statements (although the words "if" and "then" may not appear in them). *If* some fact X occurs, then some other fact Y will also occur. Investigators refer to the "if" facts as independent variables and the "then" facts as dependent variables. The dependent variable is the fact that you are explaining; the independent variable is the fact that you are assuming is influencing the dependent variable. Researchers refer to these facts as variables because it is the variation of each that interests them. Strictly speaking, hypotheses state associations, not cause/effect relationships, which are very difficult to prove in political science and sociology. It does aid understanding, however, to think of the independent variable as the cause and the dependent variable as the effect.

INDEPENDENT VARIABLE   DEPENDENT VARIABLE
        Income   →   Voting

The variation in the independent variable from citizen to citizen means that it may explain the dependent variable. If all citizens had the same income, differences in voter turnout could not be due to variations in people's income.

When stating a hypothesis, you are not attempting to persuade others but to state a tendency that must be so if the theory from which the hypothesis is drawn is true. (We will say more later about the relationship between hypotheses and theories of human behavior.) When you are writing to persuade, you have failed if the audience heeds the call of your opponents. However, if your objective is to advance knowledge, as it is here, you have "won" as much when your hypothesis is not substantiated as when it is. In either case, we know more than we knew before as the result of your study. Therefore, avoid developing a vested interest in your hypothesis.

Alternative Hypotheses

Usually there is more than one possible explanation for the phenomenon you have observed. Try to think of as many explanations as possible. Some good techniques for generating alternative hypotheses are freewriting in your journal and brainstorming. Try to look at the problem within a variety of perspectives and from several points of view.

Example: You are struck by the fact that the percentage of white students in the public schools of the nation's largest cities has dropped dramatically since 1970. You formulate the following hypotheses to explain the decline:

Hypothesis #1: As court-ordered busing has increased, the percentage of whites in our cities' public schools has decreased.

Hypothesis #2: As the white birthrate has decreased, the percentage of whites in our cities' public schools has decreased.

102

Hypothesis #3: As the income of whites living in the cities has increased, the percentage of whites in our cities' public schools has decreased.

Each of these statements has the qualities of a good hypothesis. If true, each explains "white flight" from the central cities. The data will either confirm or reject each, and all the variables are measurable, i.e., number of court decrees ordering busing, changes in the birthrate, changes in income, and changes in the percentage of a school system's population that is white.

> WRITING 6.3: STATING THE HYPOTHESIS. Develop a list of three hypotheses that if true would explain the puzzling phenomenon you identified in Writing 6.2. You must state the hypothesis in terms that permit you at the end to definitely confirm or reject it. Both the independent and dependent variables must be observable and measurable.

Step 4: Operationalize the Concepts

The terms (e.g., white flight) contained in a hypothesis are concepts. Frequently used political science concepts are *authority, social class, influence, power, conflict, political system, legitimacy,* and *political efficacy.* The hypothesis posits, or asserts, a certain kind of relationship between particular concepts. The problem is that you can't directly observe concepts in the real world — they are abstractions. So how do you measure a concept? The answer is to operationalize it — to define a concept in terms that *can* be measured. You cannot measure the "authority" of the Supreme Court but you can count the number of parties who, in a given year, refused to comply with an order of the court. Your goal is to see if the observable facts that you have deduced from the hypothesis do in fact occur.

State your hypothesis in conceptual terms: "As income increases, voter turnout increases." You must now operationalize "income" and "voter turnout." Each concept usually can be operationalized in a number of ways. For income, you might select this measure: income as revealed in exit polls taken at polling places during the 1976, 1980, and 1984 presidential elections and income

103

as revealed in the 1970 and 1980 census reports (since you need the income of both voters and nonvoters). There are also indirect measures of income, such as number of telephones, televisions, and automobiles owned, and whether the person rents or owns a dwelling. "Voter turnout" is easily operationalized as the percentage of eligible voters who cast ballots in the last three presidential elections. You would need to further operationalize "eligible voter." Do you mean persons of voting age or registered voters? The two key considerations in this process are "Is the empirical referent a good surrogate, or substitute, for the concept?" and "How costly is it to measure the empirical referent?" To test the hypothesis "If a blue-collar worker is a member of a labor union, then he or she is more likely to be a Democrat than a blue-collar worker who is not a union member," you must operationalize "blue-collar worker," "union member," and "Democrat" (Conway & Feigert, 1972). Your operational definitions might be:

Blue-collar worker:	anyone employed in an unskilled, semi-skilled, or skilled labor category as defined by the Federal Bureau of the Census
Union member:	an individual who pays dues to a labor organization that engages in collective bargaining
Democrat:	anyone who says in response to a survey, "I am a Democrat"

WRITING 6.4: OPERATIONALIZING CONCEPTS. Operationalize the concepts in one of the three hypotheses you developed in Writing 6.3.

Step 5: Develop a Strategy for Testing the Hypothesis

To test your hypothesis, you must now specify the level of analysis. The level of analysis refers to publics, political officials, cities, states, regions, countries, or other groupings. To test the hypotheses "capital punishment deters murder" you must indicate whether you are analyzing the effects of capital punishment in North America, the United States, the West, California, or Los Angeles. Then obtain a representative sample of the level selected. There is no need to interview all the members of your student body if a randomly drawn sample of two hundred students will provide a basis for accurate generalization. The two hundred students become the units of analysis. When designing research, be sure that the results can be generalized to the population mentioned in the hypothesis. Your instructor can help you learn how to draw representative samples.

In the research design, you will show why you can infer that the independent variable causes the dependent variable. First, you will show that the independent variable precedes in time the dependent variable. How do you know that increases in income precede more frequent voting? How can you show that labor union membership precedes identification with the Democratic Party?

Second, you will indicate in the research design how you will know that the independent and dependent variables vary together in a consistent, nonrandom way. Establishing covariance is the easiest part of the research design because several statistical techniques are available for determining the extent to which the independent and dependent variables vary together. The most important consideration here is to design your study so that each variable has an opportunity to vary. For example, if you are interested in a relationship between union membership and political party affiliation, choose the subjects so that all possible values of the two variables are present, i.e., union member, nonunion member, Republican, Democrat. In one such study, the researcher surveyed a random sample of blue-collar workers in her town who identified with one of the two major parties (sample size 1,055). The survey was successful because she was able to fill each of the four cells with a significant number of respondents. (See Figure 6.1, page 106.)

Third, you will have to show in the design that no other variable could have caused the variations in the dependent variable. Are there other variables, such as one's parents' party identification or one's race, that cause a person to be a Democrat? Are there rival alternative hypotheses that, if true, would explain the phenomenon better than your hypothesis? For instance, challenging the hypothesis that the drop in executions since 1960 is responsible for the rise in the murder rate are the hypotheses that say changes in the ethnic composition or average age of the population or changes in political culture better explain the increase in homicides. You must also be on the lookout for spurious, or mistaken, correlations: Two phe-

Union member

	Yes	No
Republican	115	140
Democrat	489	311

Figure 6.1

nomena may always occur together, e.g., when traffic congestion increases in a country, life expectancy also increases. But common sense tells you there is probably not a causal relationship between them. What other variable could produce both traffic congestion and a rise in life expectancy? Upon reflection you realize industrialization precedes both and is probably a cause of both increased vehicular congestion in the streets and longer life expectancies. Is there a spurious correlation between the disappearance of prayer from the public schools and the rise in teenage pregnancies?

Experimentation in Political Science

The best strategy for testing your hypothesis and the only way of establishing a true cause/effect relationship is an experiment. In an experiment the researcher randomly assigns some subjects to the test group and some to the control group, then measures the dependent variable for both groups. Then the researcher applies the independent variable to the test group and again measures the dependent variable for both groups. If the test group has changed between the measurements in a different way from how the control group has changed, the difference can only be due to the administration of the independent variable. You have established a causal relationship and eliminated the possibility of any other variable influencing the dependent variable. Experiments are common in the natural sciences but not in political science. To test experimentally a hypothesis about the impact of rises in income on voting behavior would require that the researcher remove the effect of all factors except the independent variable mentioned in the hypothesis (rise in income). Manipulation of the independent variable and holding constant other factors that might influence the dependent variable are usually impossible or unethical in political research. You would have to give money to a selected group of eligible voters and see if it had the desired effect on voting. To prove experimentally that capital punishment does not deter murder would require that convicted murderers in the test group be consistently put to death while murderers in the control group be spared. For these reasons, knowledge in political science is never as firmly established as knowledge in the natural sciences.

It is appropriate here to reemphasize the value of reading previous studies carefully and noting how others addressed the problems you are encountering in developing a strategy to test your hypothesis. You are wise to adapt the methodologies of others to your own question.

Rejection and Confirmation

How do you know whether the data confirm or fail to support your hypothesis? You calculate what the probability is that the variation you have observed is due to chance. What is the probability of a coin turning up heads 50 times out of 100? Very high. Eighty times out of 100? Very low. If there is only a 5% chance or less that the variation observed is due to random distribution, we say that the results meet the test of significance. If 70% of union members are Democrats, we must reject the hypothesis of no association because, according to the probability table (found in most statistics textbooks) the probability of that happening by chance is one in a thousand. Strictly speaking, you have not confirmed the hypothesis that union membership causes workers to join the Democratic

Party. You have rejected the *null hypothesis* — the hypothesis that there is no relationship between union membership and party affiliation. Eliminating the null hypothesis in fact is all that a researcher can do.

⌈ WRITING 6.5: Develop a strategy to test the hypothesis you
⌊ selected in Writing 6.4.

Checklist for the Research Proposal

1. Statement of the topic. What is the phenomenon that puzzles you and why is it significant?
2. Review of the literature. Summarize previous research on the question that interests you.
3. Statement of the hypothesis. In a declarative, if/then format (you need not use the actual words "if" and "then"), state the relationship between independent and dependent variables you believe to be true.
4. Operationalization of the concepts. How will you measure the terms in the hypothesis? Make the abstract concrete.
5. Summary of the strategy for testing the hypothesis. Have you considered all rival alternative hypotheses? Did you avoid spurious correlations? List the steps, in sequence, that one must take to confirm or reject the hypothesis.

WRITING 6.6: Relying upon the checklist, write a research proposal of no more than 1,500 words to test the hypothesis you selected in Writing 6.4. Many instructors will not require you to go further and actually carry out the study and write a research report. The proposal, then, must be able to stand on its own. Keep in mind that your instructor should be able to hand your finished proposal to another student or professional researcher who can carry out the project without consulting you or any other source. In this respect, a research proposal is like a recipe. By following a clearly written, well-thought-out recipe, anyone should be able to produce a first-class soufflé. This is part of the magic of *method*. Just as no responsible cookbook author would publish recipes without having others try them out first, you will find it helpful to have a friend or someone else in the class read your proposal before making the final revisions. Ask the reader if he or she would need any additional information or clarification to conduct the study.

THE RESEARCH REPORT

In the research proposal you applied the first step of the scientific method, defining the problem, and presented a plan to solve that problem. To execute that plan you must apply the remaining steps of the scientific method:

1. collect the data
2. summarize the data
3. explain the data
4. deduce hypotheses for further testing.

Only then can you write the research report.

If you have been keeping a journal, you will find it a convenient place to record, summarize, explain, and reflect upon data. Scientists for centuries have used a type of journal for these purposes, often called a field notebook or project log. Charles Darwin's notebooks, for instance, were the basis for his classic work *The Origin of Species*. If you have not been keeping a journal, now is a good time to begin.

Because much of this stage of research involves action — e.g., collecting data — rather than writing, we will not ask you to complete a writing assignment at the conclusion of each step. At the end of the chapter, however, you will pull together your data and present it in the form of a research report.

Step 1: Collect the Data

In this step you actually carry out your research design. Your instructor can suggest good books on how to conduct behavioral research in political science. Because it pertains to the kinds of tables and graphs you will include in the final written product, we will emphasize here one aspect of data gathering — data classification. Our purpose is not to teach you how to construct scales (you will have to consult references on methodology for that) but to alert you to the need to choose the appropriate scale on which to display your findings. The scales are the most important part of the research report, for most of the report consists of an explanation of the information contained in the graphs and tables.

There are three types of data you can gather: nominal-scale, ordinal-scale, and interval-scale. In *nominal scales* the classifications are mutually exclusive. Two common nominal-scale dichotomies are Democrat/Republican and union member/nonunion member. They are dichotomous variables because one cannot be both a Democrat and a Republican or belong and not belong to a union at the same time. The hypothesis that union members tend to be Democrats involves two variables (union membership and political party affiliation), and each variable has two categories. There are four possible combinations, or types. Thus this sort of nominal scale is called a typology. Researchers use cross-tabulations to analyze nominal variables. Cross-tabulations show how frequently various combinations of the dependent and independent variable occur. The number of responses or subjects in each category is placed in a cell. Your hypothesis predicts that the cell "Republican union member" would be relatively empty and the cell "Democrat union member" would be relatively full. Table 1 confirms your expectations. It shows that blue-collar workers tend to be Democrats (76% v. 24%), tend to belong to a union (57% v. 43%), and that union members are more likely to identify with the Democratic Party than nonunion members (81% v. 69%).

Table 1. *Party Identification of Blue-Collar Workers, by Union Membership*

Union Member	Party Identification		Total
	Democrat	Republican	
Yes	489 (81%)	115 (19%)	604 (57%)
No	311 (69%)	140 (31%)	451 (43%)
Total	800 (76%)	255 (24%)	1,005 (100%)

Ordinal-scale data indicate a continuum rather than a dichotomy underlying a given variable. Here we are not interested in whether someone identifies with the Republican or Democratic Party but in the strength, or degree, of that identification. Voters may describe themselves as Strong Republicans, Weak Republicans, Independent Republicans, or Independents. Any variable, such as party identification or level of knowledge, that can be categorized as low, medium, or high may be measured on an ordinal scale. Table 2 below employs an ordinal scale. It shows that more knowledgeable citizens are much more tolerant of political demonstrations than less informed citizens and that the more knowledgeable people are, the more tolerant they tend to become. For example, only 33% of respondents with very little knowledge are tolerant of demonstrations for integrated housing as opposed to 76% of highly informed respondents.

Table 2. *Percentage of Prairie City Residents Tolerating Political Demonstrations, by Level of Political Knowledge*

	Percent Tolerant			
	Level of Political Knowledge			
Demonstrations	Very Low	Low	High	Very High
By black militants	48%	51%	63%	76%
By radical students	45	48	65	76
For legalized marijuana	24	31	40	64
For integrated housing	33	47	58	76

Interval-scale data, like ordinal data, assume an underlying continuum but also have equal distances, or intervals, between classifications. If income is one of your definitions, you could classify persons according to equal intervals of $5,000: $5,001–$10,000, $10,001–$15,000, $15,001–$20,000, $20,001–$25,000, and so forth. It is also possible to construct such a scale if level of education, percent voting by districts, or expenditure on a government program is a variable. To construct an interval scale there must be a common unit of measurement underlying the continuum. Party identification can only be measured on a nominal or ordinal scale because there is no way of showing that the difference between "Independent" and "Weak Democrat" is less than the distance between "Weak Democrat" and "Strong Democrat."

Ordinal scales are more precise than nominal scales, and interval scales are more precise than ordinal scales. Political science research does not as frequently employ interval scale data, however, because of the difficulty of identifying a common unit of measurement. Nominal and ordinal data can tell us only the degree to which variables are related. Interval data permit mapping in two-dimensional space, on a scattergram, and allow us to describe the form of the relationship between the independent and dependent variables. After gathering the data for several states needed to test the hypothesis "As per capita income increases, voting turnout in presidential elections increases," we can construct a scattergram. It will tell us whether an increase in income is accompanied by an increase in voting turnout. Table 3 tells us very little. In order to see whether there is a relationship between income and voting turnout, we have transferred the data in Table 3 to Figure 6.2. Each dot is a state. By drawing a line (known as a regression line) such that half of the states are on one side and half on the other, we can see that the tendency is for voting turnout to rise as income rises. The scattergram also identifies deviant cases, i.e., states that do not fit the typical pattern. The farther from the regression line a dot is, the

Table 3.   *Per Capita Income and Voting Turnout for Selected States*

State	Income	%Turnout
1	$7830	57.0
2	7270	43.1
3	6920	53.2
4	6690	40.1
5	7000	44.9
6	6490	33.7
7	6890	54.1
8	6880	51.7
9	6780	36.2
10	7290	54.5
11	6710	50.4
12	6940	47.9

Scattergram and Regression Line for Voting Turnout (Y Axis) and Per Capita Income (X Axis)

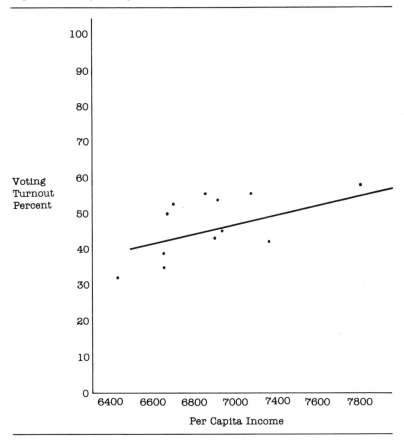

Figure 6.2 *Scattergram and regression line for voting turnout (Y axis) and per capita income (X axis)*

more anomalous or deviant it is. The researcher can then examine the anomalies to see why the hypothesis does not hold there. For a complete explanation of how to construct a scattergram, see your instructor or consult a good methodology text such as Shively (1974).

113

Step 2: Summarize the Data

The next step in scientific research is to summarize the data you have collected. As you follow the research design you will wish to record the data in an accountable manner so that they can be reproduced if necessary. In your journal or project log, record the data, document the steps of the research design, note any deviations from the design in the execution of the study, and reflect upon the data. For example, if your research proposal called for a random sample of blue-collar workers in your town but, because of time and cost restraints, you had to draw your sample from the workers in a single factory, you will note this change in the log.

Beware of the tendency of researchers to assign an almost sacrosanct character to the data. Because numbers are abstractions from observable phenomena, they can yield a false sense of precision. For instance, a researcher surveying public opinion on whether prostitution should be legalized will likely reduce all responses, no matter how complex or qualified, to two categories — yes and no.

The best way to summarize nominal and ordinal data is in a table. A scattergram is the preferred format for the presentation of interval data.

Step 3: Explain the Data

Next, you explain in tabular form the data you have summarized. You will attempt to answer a "why" question. Why do middle-class citizens vote in higher percentages than working-class citizens? Why do union members tend to be Democrats? Why has the percentage of Americans describing themselves as Independents increased? You must go beyond the mere assertion of correlation between variables to an explanation for the correlation you have discovered. The goal of the scientific study of politics is not merely to describe political phenomena but to explain and predict political behavior. Explanation and prediction are logically the same. The difference between them refers to the time of occurrence, past or future. If you can explicate why some countries are politically stable and others are not, you should be able to predict how stable a particular nation will be.

114

To explain and predict, you will draw upon laws and theories. A hypothesis tested many times and not rejected is a law. A theory is a group of laws. Laws explain the individual facts; theories explain laws. From theories one can deduce hypotheses, which when successfully tested yield new laws and extensions of existing theory. Theories guide the research process. Explanation occurs when the researcher can deduce the facts to be explained as a logical consequence of the laws or theory. According to a well-established theory, liquids become solids when the temperature falls below a substance's freezing point. We know that the freezing point of water is 0° Centigrade. If we place a glass of water outside when the temperature is −10° C, we can deduce from the theory that the water in the glass will freeze. If the people of a district with a major river that regularly floods elect someone to Congress, we can deduce from the law of logrolling that that legislator will become a champion for federal water projects not only in his or her home district and but in other districts as well. We have explained the variation in the dependent variable (voting behavior) and independent variable (hydrographic nature of district) by bringing the variation under a general theory (logrolling).

The goal of observation and measurement is sounder scientific laws and better empirical theories. Although we can know a fact to be true we can never know a theory to be entirely true. That the sun rose today is a fact. "The sun rises every 24 hours" is a theoretical statement and would be disproven if the sun failed to rise tomorrow morning.

To explain your data you will probably draw upon one of the following theories of political behavior. Your instructor can point you to fuller treatments of each. According to the *psychological approach* political behavior is the result of individual attitudes or personalities. For instance, conservative judges decide differently from liberal judges. *Game theory* assumes that human beings are rational actors and seek to win. All other things being equal, Supreme Court justices prefer to be in the majority than in the minority in the disposition of a case. The *economic model* also assumes rationality but regards decisions as the outcome of cost/benefit analysis. *Role theory* posits that actors' concepts of the nature of the office determine their behavior. Thus, judges who believe the

115

judicial role is to interpret law and the legislature's role is to make law will uphold criminal convictions even if they think the law the criminal was charged with violating is foolish. *Group-level analysis* focuses upon the dynamics of group interaction. Because the Supreme Court is a small group, bargaining among the justices accounts for at least some of their decisions. *Systems theory* observes that political institutions and actors operate within a system. Researchers study inputs into the system (interest group demands, public opinion), relationships within the system (Senate and House of Representatives), outputs of the system (decisions and policies), and feedback, or the influence of outputs on inputs and thus on decisions. *Communications theory* assumes that we can only understand the workings of the political system if we understand the messages and the communication facilities that belong to it. Focus is on the sending, receiving, and storing of messages, e.g., Supreme Court opinions are messages to attentive publics, and editorial writers are members of the attentive public who react to these messages by sending messages of their own to the general public and to the Court.

Let us present some examples of potentially good explanations for the data presented in Tables 1, 2, and 3. Why are union members much more likely to identify with the Democratic Party than nonunion blue-collar workers? The psychological approach would suggest that both the inclination to join a union and to identify with the Democratic Party are functions of basic *attitudes* that precede joining a union or a party. The economic model hints that union members *calculate* that they will gain more benefits than costs from support for Democratic candidates. Role theory suggests that union membership carries with it an *expectation* of affiliation with the Democratic Party. As you can see, there are usually several possible theoretical explanations for any given set of data. Choose the one which you think best accounts for the variation you have observed. Why are better informed people more tolerant of political demonstrations? The obvious importance of attitudes here points to the psychological approach as a good source of explanation. Why is high income associated with voter turnout? Is it because members of the middle class have different attitudes toward civic duty or greater feelings of political efficacy than the poor and working class, or is it because they are better educated? Or is it because middle-class individuals discern a potential reward for political involvement and a potential penalty for political apathy? The former question suggests the psychological approach or role theory, and the latter the economic model.

Step 4: Deduce Further Hypotheses for Testing

The final step in the scientific method is to deduce from your explanation further hypotheses for testing. Any explanation, because it is drawn from a general theory of human behavior, covers more than the original set of facts. Political scientists, indeed, are adept at seeing the political implications of theories originated in other sciences. Most of the theoretical approaches to political analysis mentioned in the previous section were developed in disciplines other than political science. For instance, the father of communications analysis is a physicist and mathematician, Norbert Wiener. Psychologists pioneered in the theories of personality and attitudes. Social psychologists developed the first laws of small-group dynamics, and we are indebted to economists for the cost/benefit approach.

The ramifications of your explanation may not be readily apparent. By persistent deduction, however, you can extract the logical implications and then select one or more hypotheses for testing. The explanation thus provides the topic of investigation we began with in step 1. This is the continuous cycle of the scientific process, and this is what makes the development and extension of scientific theories possible. A researcher who confirmed the hypothesis that as races mix in the public schools racial bigotry will decline might, as an explanation, point to the principle that prejudice is the result of ignorance. Looking for other implications of this principle, the researcher might posit the hypothesis that the more frequent the cultural exchanges between two countries or the greater the volume of mail that passes across borders the less likely is war between them. What hypotheses can you deduce from your explanation for why levels of income are associated with voter turnout? If the theory you rely upon is that human beings are rational actors and that the middle class and the rich have more at stake in governmental decision making, you have a rich source of interesting hypotheses. If people are rational actors, shouldn't capital punishment deter

117

murder? If you rely upon attitudinal explanations, you could deduce the hypothesis that democracy is more likely to exist and to
succeed in relatively wealthy countries.

> WRITING 7.7: After executing a research proposal, pre-
> pared by you or someone else, present your findings in the form
> of a research report less than 3,000 words long. Remember that
> the report is a type of expository essay and should possess all
> the qualities of good exposition. Be sure to follow the checklist
> as you write.

Checklist for the Research Report

1. Statement of the thesis. The purpose of the essay is to support
   the thesis, or conclusion. The thesis will be that the hypothesis
   you tested was either confirmed or rejected. Enumerate the assumptions of your study.
2. Present the data in tables and graphs and explain them. A common error of student writers is to believe that the figures speak
   for themselves. This is not so. The tables are merely numbers.
   The terms, propositions, and arguments contained in the nar-
   rative give meaning to the numbers.
3. Explain the data by reference to a law or theory. What predictions does your hypothesis permit you to make?
4. From the law or theory deduce one or more hypotheses for
   further testing. How will testing them advance the theory or
   law?

[7] Principles of Research and Basic Bibliographies

PREVIEW: *If only you knew what your college library contains! Whenever you have to write an issue analysis, policy analysis, research proposal, or term paper, you turn to the library. In this chapter you'll learn — step-by-step — just how to find the information you need.*

Select a topic
Consult reference works for background information
Make a list of subject headings
Consult indexes, abstracts, and bibliographies and prepare bibliography cards
Read and take notes on appropriate books and articles
The researcher's sources

The rapid development of knowledge in the centuries since the Renaissance can be attributed to two factors: a pervasive spirit of inquiry and the system of incrementally adding to the store of existing knowledge. To exploit this knowledge explosion, however, you must first master the skills of library research.

Your instructor has asked you to write a paper requiring library research. This may be a research report (Chapter 6), an issue analysis (Chapter 4), a policy analysis (Chapter 5), or a traditional term paper. If you follow the process approach, which is the strategy of this book, you will complete the project on time and enjoy yourself as well. In this chapter we discuss the steps that prepare you to write the paper. In most cases, you will need to complete each step in sequence. If your topic is one on which you already have a good deal of information, the first three steps will be easy.

The preparatory, or research, stage of the writing process consists of five steps:

1.   Select a topic.
2.   Consult reference works for background information.
3.   Make a list of subject headings.
4.   Consult indexes, abstracts, and bibliographies and prepare bibliography cards.
5.   Read and take notes on appropriate books and articles.

Step 1: Select a Topic

Begin by reviewing class notes and assigned readings. Your textbooks can be very useful at the beginning of a project. Is there a subject that particularly interests you? Phrase your interest in the form of a research topic or question to which you are seeking an answer. Avoid topics that are so broad that the research materials will overwhelm you, as well as overly narrow topics on which little information is available. Here is an example of each type:

Too broad: "Apartheid in South Africa."

Although this is a very interesting subject, you will not be able to manage the mass of materials relating to apartheid, and your treatment of it will be superficial and unimpressive to the reader.

Too narrow: "The Racial Integration of the Johannesburg Traffic Police."

The key difficulty here is the absence of a sufficient quantity of published material to permit any informed conclusions on the subject. Also, as topics become narrower they tend to lose reader appeal.

Good: "Bishop Desmond Tutu's Case for a Strategy of Nonviolent Protest To End Apartheid in South Africa."

On this topic there are documents and speeches as well as a sufficient quantity of commentary and analysis on which to base a solid paper. Although perhaps not as interesting as the first topic, it is more manageable and still interesting enough to keep the reader's attention.

When selecting a topic, keep in mind that you will want to reach a conclusion or judgment and cast it as your paper's thesis. Do not expect simply to summarize your research or describe your subject. As you are completing each step, draft a tentative thesis and expect to revise it as your research progresses. Initially, for example, you may think that nonviolence will not produce results in South Africa, but as you become increasingly familiar with the case for this approach and against the alternatives to it you may re-examine your position. You do not need to reach a firm conclusion until the research is complete and you are ready to write the paper.

Step 2: Consult Reference Works for Background Information

Your textbooks and class notes may provide you with little or no information about your topic. Before you can utilize any of the finding aids discussed below, you will need to develop at least a superficial knowledge of the persons, facts, events, and controversies relevant to the subject. Your first look at the topic is thus very important. Depending on your topic, you may not need to use all of the suggested sources of background information. Political science students find the following reference works to be good places to get an initial overview:

A. Political Science Encyclopedias and Dictionaries

These are the best places to get that first look. Entries are brief but to the point. Encyclopedias contain essays on topics; dictionaries offer definitions of terms. The encyclopedia with the best essays on political topics is:

> *International encyclopedia of the social sciences* (1968). New York: Macmillan.

A student writing on the concept of law imbedded in the Declaration of Independence would want to read the essay on "Natural Law," while one investigating the justness of the free market would begin on the right foot by perusing the entries under "Capitalism" and "Marxism." Some of the articles are dated, such as the one on "Foundations," but the essays on concepts, such as "Poverty" and "Equality," and the biographical articles are excellent.

Political science, like other academic disciplines, possesses a specialized vocabulary. (Critics refer to it as jargon.) One of the secrets to success in political science courses is to master unfamiliar terms. As you read encyclopedia essays and other sources in preparation for completing a writing assignment you will probably encounter new words or words that have a special meaning to political scientists. Good sources of definitions for such terms are:

> Plano, J. C., & Greenberg, M. (1982). *The American political dictionary* (6th ed.). New York: Holt, Rinehart and Winston.

The series of dictionaries published by American Bibliographic Center — Clio Press, Santa Barbara, California are

> Plano, J. C., & Olton, R. (1982). *The international relations dictionary* (3d ed.).

> Plano, J. C., et al. (1982). *The dictionary of political analysis* (2nd ed.).

> Phillips, C. S. (1983). *The African political dictionary.*

> Rossi, E. E. & Plano, J. C. (1981). *The Latin American political dictionary.*

> Rossi, E. E., & McCrea, B. (1985). *The European political dictionary.*

> Ziring, L. (1982). *The Middle East dictionary.*

> Ziring, L. (1985). *The Asian political dictionary.*

Each dictionary identifies people, events, terms, and concepts significant in the treated subfield. Your topic will dictate which dictionary to consult. If you encounter the unfamiliar term "*laissez-faire,*" for instance, while reading about President Roosevelt's attempt to "pack" the U.S. Supreme Court in 1937, you would look it up in *The American political dictionary.* For some topics you may find more than one dictionary pertinent.

B. Biographical Dictionaries and Directories

In your reading you will often see references to men, women, and organizations with which you are unfamiliar. An article about South Africa, for example, might mention Bishop Tutu, someone unknown to you. A convenient way of learning more about such individuals is to consult one of the following works:

> *Who's Who in Government* (1972/73--). Chicago: Marquis Who's Who.

Provides information on officials in federal, state, local, and foreign governments. Updated biennially.

> *Official Congressional Directory* (1982--). Washington, D.C.: Government Printing Office.

Contains a wide range of information about members of Congress, including addresses. Useful for students wishing to write a letter to their representative or senator.

> *United States Government Manual* (1935--). Washington, D.C.: Government Printing Office.

Published each year. Here you will find the address and telephone number as well as a description of each department and agency in the federal government.

> *Encyclopedia of Associations* (1956--). Detroit: Gale Research Co.

Published every two years. Describes almost 20,000 organizations and associations and provides their addresses.

If you were analyzing a congressional hearing investigating the Environmental Protection Agency's administration of the Superfund clean-up program, you could use these dictionaries and directories to identify and characterize the members of the committee, the witnesses who testified, and the associations they represent.

C. Guides to Reference Works in Political Science

If you do not know where to go to get a brief introduction to your subject, three very useful places to begin your research project are:

> Sheehy, E. P. (1976). *Guide to reference books* (9th ed.). Chicago: American Library Association.

Supplemented in 1980 and 1982. The section on political science identifies and annotates the most important guides, bibliographies, dictionaries, encyclopedias, directories, handbooks, tables, biographies, and yearbooks in the discipline.

> Holler, F. L. (1981). *The information sources of political science* (3d ed.). Santa Barbara, CA: American Bibliographic Center — Clio Press.

Holler divides political science into the following five subfields:

1. American government.
2. International relations.
3. Comparative politics.
4. Political theory.
5. Public administration.

He divides each of these subfields into topics and lists the major reference works, such as encyclopedias and dictionaries, available under each topic. A student wishing to write an essay on the social welfare policy of West Germany could begin by consulting the "comparative and area studies" section of Holler.

> Vose, C. E. (1975). *A guide to library sources in political science: American government.* Washington, D.C.: The American Political cal Science Association.

The author compares various reference sources such as encyclopedias, dictionaries, and almanacs with regard to specific topics.

Step 3: Make a List of Subject Headings

While you are having that first look at your subject, make a list of subject headings. These headings are specific subtopics included within your general topic. You will need these in order to make use of the finding aids described in step 4, because articles and books are indexed according to subject headings. Without these headings you will be unable to locate books, articles, or documents. Your list should cover all aspects of your topic. State your subtopics in as many ways as possible because all the finding aids do not employ the same subject headings. For instance, if your topic were the role of the Senate in the formulation of treaties, you would find useful titles in periodical indexes, card catalogs, and bibliographies under the following headings:

> Treaty-Making Power — United States

United States — Foreign Relations — Treaties
United States — Congress — Senate

The best source of card catalog subject headings is:

U.S. Library of Congress (1980). *Library of Congress subject headings* (9th ed.). Washington, D.C.: Library of Congress.

This work is supplemented quarterly with annual accumulations. It is a good place to begin your search for subject headings, because it will tell you what the card catalog calls your subject. You will also need a list of subject headings to conduct a computer search for sources. If your headings are too general, the computer printout will run several pages and list many titles not relevant to your paper. Precise headings are the key to successful use of this resource.

Step 4: Consult Indexes, Abstracts, and Bibliographies and Prepare Bibliography Cards

Equipped with a list of subject headings, you are now ready to utilize a number of aids for finding relevant articles and books. Keep a record on 4" × 6" cards of how you used each of these sources. This record will prevent redoing work already done once. Each search card should look something like Figure 7.1.

Public Affairs Information Service Bulletin
Volumes used: v. 70 (1984) to v. 71 (1985)
Topic: Are churches that provide sanctuary to Guatemalan and Salvadoran refugees breaking the law?
Headings Used:
  Asylum, Right of
  Refugees, Political
  Refugees, Guatemalan
  Refugees, Salvadoran
  Refugees, Central America

Figure 7.1

125

A. Political Science Journal Indexes and Abstracts

One of the best sources for political science research is articles in political science journals. They are more current than books and often contain information that may never appear in book form. To use these articles, however, one must know how to find them. The four best tools for locating relevant articles are:

> ABC Pol Sci: Advanced Bibliography of Contents, Political Science and Government (1969--). Santa Barbara, CA: American Bibliographic Center — Clio Press.

Comes out eight times a year and contains law and court decision indexes as well as general political science subject and author indexes.

> Public Affairs Information Service (1915--). *Bulletin.* New York: PAIS.

Appears weekly and indexes over 1,000 periodicals in the social sciences.

> *Social Sciences Index* (1974--). New York: Wilson.

Published four times a year.

> *Social Sciences Citation Index* (1973--). Philadelphia: Institute for Scientific Information.

Published three times a year. If you think you have located a seminal article that might be cited in subsequent research, consult the *Social Sciences Citation Index* for a list of recent articles citing that work. For example, your topic is delay in the courts. You are trying to understand why litigants in some courts wait, on the average, three years for their case to come to trial, while in other courts they need wait only six months. You believe that the best piece of research on this subject is a 1975 article published in volume 9 of *Law & Society Review* beginning on p. 321 by Joel Grossman and Austin Sarat entitled "Litigation in the Federal Courts: A Comparative Perspective." You believe that scholars who cite this essay in their published work might have something to contribute to an understanding of this issue. To identify these articles you simply consult the latest edition of the *Social Sciences Citation Index* under the name of the first author "GROSSMAN JB" and there you find references to two 1983 scholarly articles, by D. M. Engel and W. McIntosh, as shown in Figure 7.2.

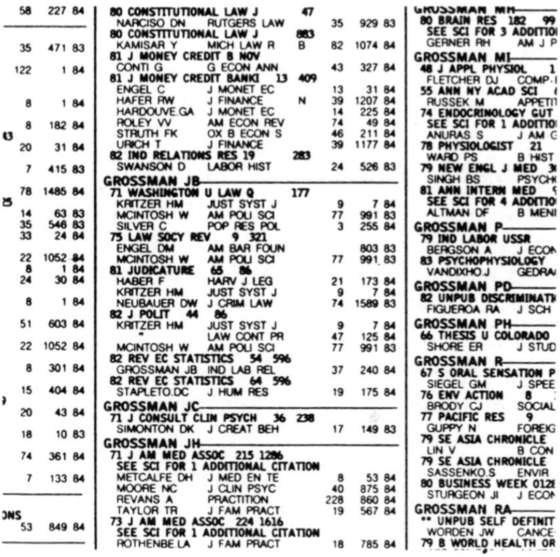

58 227 84
35 471 83
122 1 84
8 1 84
8 182 84
20 31 84
7 415 83
78 1485 84
14 63 83
35 546 83
33 24 84
22 1052 84
8 1 84
24 30 84
8 1 84
51 603 84
22 1052 84
8 301 84
15 404 84
20 43 84
18 10 83
74 361 84
7 133 84
53 849 84

80 CONSTITUTIONAL LAW J 47
NARCISO DN RUTGERS LAW 35 929 83
80 CONSTITUTIONAL LAW J 883
KAMISAR Y MICH LAW R B 82 1074 84
81 J MONEY CREDIT B NOV
CONTI G G ECON ANN 43 327 84
81 J MONEY CREDIT BANKI 13 409
ENGEL C J MONET EC 13 31 84
HAFER RW J FINANCE N 39 1207 84
HARDOUVE.GA J MONET EC 14 225 84
ROLEY VV AM ECON REV 74 49 84
STRUTH FK OX B ECON S 46 211 84
URICH T J FINANCE 39 1177 84
82 IND RELATIONS RES 19 283
SWANSON D LABOR HIST 24 526 83
GROSSMAN JB
71 WASHINGTON U LAW Q 177
KRITZER HM JUST SYST J 9 7 84
MCINTOSH W AM POLI SCI 77 991 83
SILVER C POP RES POL 3 255 84
75 LAW SOCY REV 9 321
ENGEL DM AM BAR FOUN 803 83
MCINTOSH W AM POLI SCI 77 991 83
81 JUDICATURE 65 86
HABER F HARV J LEG 21 173 84
KRITZER HM JUST SYST J 9 7 84
NEUBAUER DW J CRIM LAW 74 1589 83
82 J POLIT 44 86
KRITZER HM JUST SYST J 9 7 84
" LAW CONT PR 47 125 84
MCINTOSH W AM POLI SCI 77 991 83
82 REV EC STATISTICS 54 596
GROSSMAN JB IND LAB REL 37 240 84
82 REV EC STATISTICS 64 596
STAPLETO.DC J HUM RES 19 175 84
GROSSMAN JC
71 J CONSULT CLIN PSYCH 36 238
SIMONTON DK J CREAT BEH 17 149 83
GROSSMAN JH
71 J AM MED ASSOC 215 1286
SEE SCI FOR 1 ADDITIONAL CITATION
METCALFE DH J MED EN TE 8 53 84
MOORE NC J CLIN PSYC 40 875 84
REVANS A PRACTITION 228 860 84
TAYLOR TR J FAM PRACT 19 567 84
73 J AM MED ASSOC 224 1616
SEE SCI FOR 1 ADDITIONAL CITATION
ROTHENBE.LA J FAM PRACT 18 785 84

GROSSMAN MH
80 BRAIN RES 182 99
SEE SCI FOR 3 ADDITIO
GERNER RH AM J P
GROSSMAN MI
48 J APPL PHYSIOL 1
FLETCHER DJ COMP-
55 ANN NY ACAD SCI
RUSSEK M APPETI
74 ENDOCRINOLOGY GUT
SEE SCI FOR 1 ADDITIO
ANURAS S J AM G
78 PHYSIOLOGIST 21
WARD PS B HIST
79 NEW ENGL J MED
SINGH BS PSYCH
81 ANN INTERN MED
SEE SCI FOR 4 ADDITIO
ALTMAN DF B MENI
GROSSMAN P
79 IND LABOR USSR
BERGSON A J ECON
83 PSYCHOPHYSIOLOGY
VANDIXHO.J GEDRA
GROSSMAN PD
82 UNPUB DISCRIMINATI
FIGUEROA RA J SCH
GROSSMAN PH
66 THESIS U COLORADO
SHORE ER J STUD
GROSSMAN R
67 S ORAL SENSATION P
SIEGEL GM J SPEE
76 ENV ACTION 8
BRODY CJ SOCIAL
77 PACIFIC RES 9
GUPPY N FOREIG
79 SE ASIA CHRONICLE
LIN V B CON
79 SE ASIA CHRONICLE
SASSENKO.S ENVIR
80 BUSINESS WEEK 012
STURGEON JI J ECON
GROSSMAN RA
** UNPUB SELF DEFINIT
WORDEN JW CANCE
79 B WORLD HEALTH OR

Figure 7.2

Abstracts are often more useful than periodical indexes because they contain summaries of each article as well as its citation. You can discover by a quick perusal of the abstract whether you need to go to the trouble of finding the article itself. Political scientists use four abstracts most frequently:

> *International Political Science Abstracts* (1951--). Oxford: Basil Blackwell.

Published every two months. Contains abstracts of about 200 words for each article cited.

> *America: History and Life* (1964-65--). Santa Barbara, CA: American Bibliographic Center — Clio Press.

Contains briefer descriptions of the contents of the articles listed.

Political Science Abstracts (1967--). New York: Plenum.

Summarizes thousands of books, articles, and documents in each subfield of the discipline.

United States Political Science Documents (USPSD) (1975). Pittsburgh, PA.: University of Pittsburgh Press.

Part 1 is an index, and Part 2 abstracts the articles cited in the index.

For any topic in political science, break it down into subject headings and use these indexes and abstracts to compile a list of articles that you will want to investigate. For example, let us assume that you wish to write a research report that tests the hypothesis that as split-ticket balloting increases in the United States the level of party identification decreases. After getting a first look at the subject but before going to the indexes, you draw up the following list of subject headings: Split-ticket voting, Ticket-splitting, Voting behavior, Elections, Electoral behavior, Political parties, Party loyalty, and Party identification. You go to the subject index in a recent issue of *International Political Science Abstracts*. You immediately notice that your subject headings are inadequate because they do not reflect the fact that you are interested only in American elections. So you revise them by putting "United States of America" before each one. You find nothing germane under these headings: "United States of America — split-ticket voting," "United States of America — ticket-splitting," "United States of America — voting behavior," and "United States of America — elections." However, on p. 568 under "United States of America — electoral behavior" you find the entry shown in Figure 7.3.

You then turn to p. 89 of the abstracts section, which organizes the abstracts in numerical order. The 996th abstract listed is the following:

34. 996   GITELSON, Alan R; RICHARD, Patricia Bayer —
          Ticket-splitting: aggregate measures vs. actual ballots.
          Western Political Quarterly 36(3). Sept. 83: 410–419.

In recent years the phenomenon of ticket-splitting has captured the attention not only of political scientists but of political practitioners as well.

(United States of America, elections, presidential)
    home state advantage : 1071
        mortality rate : 2771
        negative support : 5280
        newspapers, foreign policy, edito-
            rials : 2688
        prediction : 4316
        primary : 2672
            1976 : 912
            1980 : 1242
    racial crossover voting : 4571
    senatorial
        1974-1978, competition, and consti-
            tuencies : 888
        and congressional, 1920-1980 : 4655
        and state population : 2608
        incumbents : 1230
        re-election chances : 4693
    Two-Party Index : 4319
    write-in campaigns : 2567
    Georgia, 1970-1978, women : 3730
    Iowa, political parties, 1980, caucu-
        ses : 2755
    New Mexico, women : 3704
    Oklahoma, women : 3716
    electoral behavior : 334, 1275, 2738
        1824-1970, nationalization : 3703
        1914-1980 : 1231
        Blacks : 1275
            newspapers : 1061
            Chicago : 1275
        civil service : 3683
        elections, presidential, primary, 1980:
            1242
        environmental problems : 646
        farmers : 3849
        Indians, Arizona : 1104
        misreporting : 5035
        rationality : 4595
        social class : 3706
    →ticket-splitting : 996
        New York State, ballot non-completion :
            2679
    electoral law, Voting Rights Act, 1964-
        1975 : 2406
    electoral participation : 1272, 4289
        Blacks, Chicago : 935
        elections
            gubernatorial : 1153

Figure 7.3

129

The study of split-ticket voting, however, has been confined to the use of indirect measures, primarily survey and aggregate data, because of the un-availability of actual ballots. The researchers examine several aggregate measures of ticket-splitting which have been proposed and/or employed in the literature. We then evaluate the accuracy of these aggregate measures by comparing the estimates of ticket-splitting with actual ticket-splitting in one [US] community, ascertained from its 1972 and 1976 election ballots (computer punch cards). Evidence presented in this paper provides empirical substantiation for criticism of the aggregate measures of ticket-splitting. Researchers who use measures proposed by Burnham and Duncan and Davis must be careful in the claims built upon them. [R]

This is an article that has direct bearing on your hypothesis, so you will want to locate it and read it carefully. What if you had started, not with the *International Political Science Abstracts,* but with the *Social Sciences Index?* You would still have identified the Gitelson and Richard piece but the steps would have been different. First, you would notice that the scope of the *Social Sciences Index* is primarily American, so it is not necessary to go to the entry "United States." Under your first subject heading, "split-ticket voting" you find nothing, but under the second, "ticket-splitting," you find the following notation on p. 1234:

> Ticket-splitting. See Independent voting

You then turn to p. 575, where you find this citation:

> Independent voting
> Ticket-splitting: aggregate measures vs. actual ballot.
> A. R. Gitelson and P. B. Richard. bibl W Pol Q 36:410–
> 19 S '83

Note that there are no annotations describing the contents of the article. The reason is that here you are using an index rather than an abstract.

B. Political Science Bibliographies

You will want to find not only journal articles but also books on your topic. A bibliography is a very useful aid in finding books.

Four of the most widely used bibliographies in political science research are:

> *Foreign Affairs Bibliography* (1933--). New York: Council on Foreign Relations.

Published every ten years. An effective finding aid for students of international relations. Provides a brief description of each book listed.

> *International Bibliography of Political Science* (1953--). Paris: UNESCO.

Issued annually. Covers books and articles published in each subfield of the discipline.

> Hall, K. L. (1984). *Bibliography of American constitutional and legal history, 1896–1979.* Millwood, N. Y.: Kraus International Publications, 5 vols.

An excellent source of works on constitutional and legal doctrine as well as a guide to judicial biographies. A student writing on congressional attempts to curb the Supreme Court or on John Marshall could not find a better place to begin.

> Englefield, D., & Drewry, G. (Eds.) (1984). *Information sources in politics and political science: A survey worldwide.* London: Butterworth.

Although containing some references to articles, most of this work consists of annotated bibliographies. It covers six approaches to the study of politics and government and the politics and government of all major countries and regions of the world. The British politics section is especially strong.

C. The Card Catalog

Another means for identifying books pertaining to your topic is to consult your library's card catalog, which if computerized does not consist of cards at all. You will also need to use the card catalog to find books you have identified from bibliographies. Each book the library owns is listed here in three ways: by title, by author, and by subject. If you know the title or author of a book you want, simply find the book card, which shows the call number. The call number assigned to each book is unique — no other book in the collection has that number. That number tells you where to find the book on the shelves. A few libraries have closed stacks, denying students access to the shelves. In a closed-stack library you fill out a call slip and present it to a librarian, who will get the book for you. If you are not looking for a specific book but want to see what is available on your topic, you need to check the subject catalog. Of course, you will first have to identify relevant subject headings (see step 3). Look up the topic ("judicial review," for example) and you will probably find a number of books listed. Be sure to include the call number on a bibliography card for each book that looks valuable. In general, published bibliographies are more reliable sources of books on a particular topic than library card catalogs. Card catalogs, however, are more up-to-date than most bibliographies, so make it a practice to use both sources when seeking books. Say your topic is the influence of the communications media on presidential elections. Your first subject heading is "presidential elections." When you go to the subject section of the card catalog, the only card you find is the one in Figure 7.4.

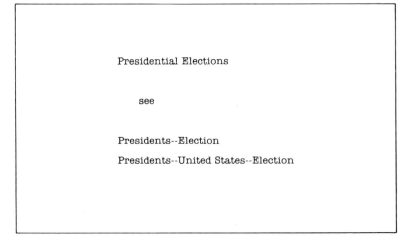

Figure 7.4

Accordingly, you then consult the catalog subject heading "presidents — United States — election" and find a number of cards. Figure 7.5 shows one.

```
                PRESIDENTS--UNITED STATES--ELECTION
324
.70973      Arterton, F. Christopher.
Ar75m           Media politics : the news strategies
            of presidential campaigns / F.
            Christopher Arterton. — Lexington,
            Mass. : Lexington Books, c 1984.
                xiv, 220 p. : ill. ; 24 cm.
                Includes bibliographic references
            and index.
                ISBN 0-669-07504-3 (alk. paper)


                1. Presidents--United States--
            Election.  2. Mass media--Political
            aspects--United States.  I. Title

VtU                                      VTUUsc    83-48735
```

Figure 7.5

Figures 7.6 and 7.7 (p. 134) show the author and title card for this book. These cards are filed alphabetically and contain much usable information. The most helpful are the "tracings," which provide other subject headings that may be relevant to your topic.

Prepare Bibliography Cards

As you locate relevant books, articles, and documents in the finding aids, prepare a 4" × 6" bibliography card for each title. Each citation must be complete in order to use interlibrary loan or to prepare a list of references to be placed at the end of your paper. For the correct citation forms see Chapter 8. Figures 7.8 and 7.9 (p. 135) are examples of bibliography cards for a book and an article.

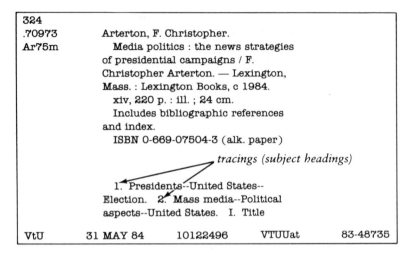

```
324
.70973        Arterton, F. Christopher.
Ar75m             Media politics : the news strategies
              of presidential campaigns / F.
              Christopher Arterton. — Lexington,
              Mass. : Lexington Books, c 1984.
                  xiv, 220 p. : ill. ; 24 cm.
                  Includes bibliographic references
              and index.
                  ISBN 0-669-07504-3 (alk. paper)

                                    tracings (subject headings)

                  1. Presidents--United States--
              Election.   2. Mass media--Political
              aspects--United States.   I. Title

   VtU        31 MAY 84        10122496      VTUUat        83-48735
```

Figure 7.6

```
              Media politics
324
.70973        Arterton, F. Christopher.
Ar75m             Media politics : the news strategies
              of presidential campaigns / F.
              Christopher Arterton. — Lexington,
              Mass. : Lexington Books, c 1984.
                  xiv, 220 p. : ill. ; 24 cm.
                  Includes bibliographic references
              and index.
                  ISBN 0-669-07504-3 (alk. paper)


                  1. Presidents--United States--
              Election.   2. Mass media--Political
              aspects--United States.   I. Title

   VtU                                      VTUUat        83-48735
```

Figure 7.7

134

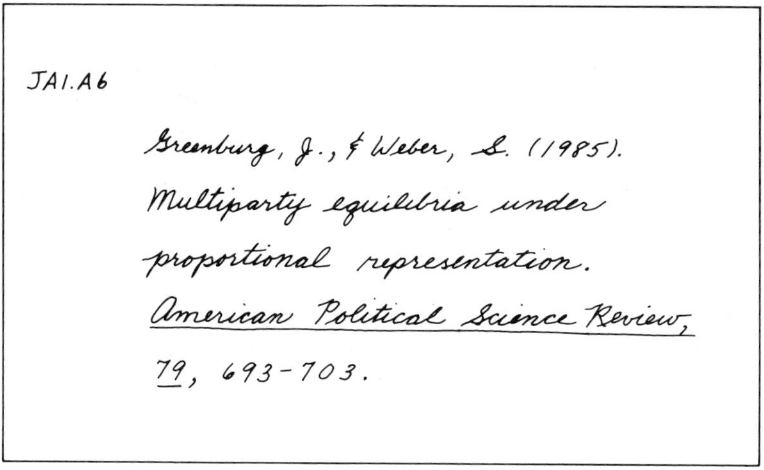

JA1.A6

Greenburg, J., & Weber, S. (1985).
Multiparty equilibria under
proportional representation.
American Political Science Review,
79, 693-703.

Figure 7.8

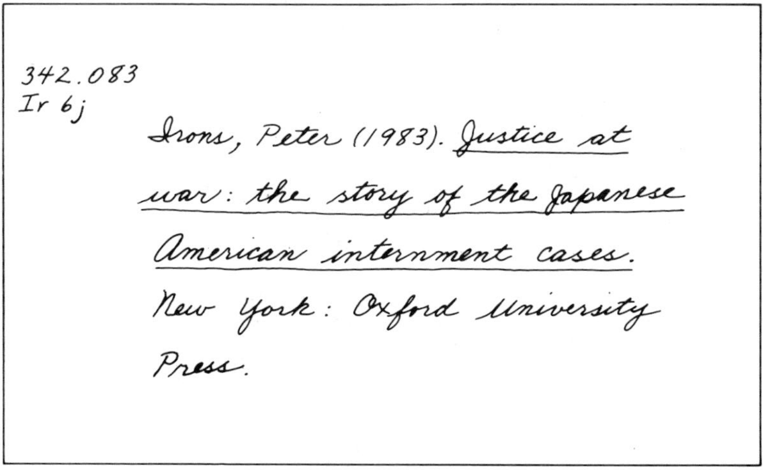

342.083
Ir 6j

Irons, Peter (1983). Justice at
war: the story of the Japanese
American internment cases.
New York: Oxford University
Press.

Figure 7.9

Cataloging Systems

As you take notes at the card catalog, you will copy the call number of each reference. The composition of that call number will depend on which of two cataloging systems your library uses: Library of Congress or Dewey decimal. Both are attempts to classify and arrange the holdings of a library and make them accessible to readers. Early in your research you will want to understand how your library's system works. Familiarity with the classification system will allow you to browse through the shelves containing books on your subject. The Library of Congress system uses the alphabet for the divisions, for example, E and F for History, H for Economics, J for Political Science, and K for Law. This system allows for finer classification by the addition of a second letter followed by numbers.

Library of Congress Classification

		Political Science
J		Official documents
		General serial documents only. For documents limited to special subjects, *see* the subject in B-Z
	1–9	Official gazettes
		United States documents
		For congressional hearings, reports, etc., *see* KF
	80–85	Presidents' messages and other executive documents
	86–87	State documents
	100–981	Other countries
		For documents issued by local governments, *see* JS
JA		Collections and general works
JC		Political theory. Theory of the state
	311–323	Nationalism. Minorities. Geopolitics
	325–341	Nature, entity, concept of the state
	345–347	Symbolism, emblems of the state: Arms, flag, seal, etc.

	Political Science	
	348–497	Forms of the state
		Including imperialism, the world state, monarchy, aristocracy, democracy, fascism, dictatorships
	501–628	Purpose, functions, and relations of the state
	571–628	The state and the individual. Individual rights. Liberty
JF		Constitutional history and administration
		General works. Comparative works
	201–723	Organs and function of government
		Including executive branch, cabinet and ministerial government, legislative bodies
	800–1191	Political rights and guarantees
		Including citizenship, suffrage, electoral systems, representation, the ballot
	1321–2112	Government. Administration
	1411–1674	Civil service
	2011–2112	Political parties
		Special countries
JK		United States
JL		British America. Latin America
JN		Europe
JQ		Asia. Africa. Australia. Oceania
JS		Local government
	3–27	Serial documents (General)
	141–231	Municipal government
	241–285	Local government other than municipal
JV		Colonies and colonization. Emigration and immigration
JX		International law. International relations
	63–1195	Collections. Documents. Cases
	101–115	Diplomatic relations (Universal collections)
	120–191	Treaties (Universal collections)

Political Science		
	1305–1598	International relations. Foreign relations For International questions treated as sources of or contributions to the theory of international law. For histories of events, diplomatic histories, etc., *see* D-F
	1625–1896	Diplomacy. The diplomatic service
	1901–1995	International arbitration. World peace. International organization Including peace movements, League of Nations, United Nations, arbitration treaties, international courts
	2001–5810	International law (Treaties and monographs)

Law		
K		Law (General)
	237–487	Jurisprudence. Philosophy and theory of law
	540–5570	Comparative law. International uniform law
	7051–7720	Conflict of laws
		Law of the United Kingdom and Ireland
KD		Law of England and Wales
	8850–9312	Local laws of England
	9320–9355	Local laws of Wales
	9400–9500	Law of Wales
KDC		Law of Scotland
KDE		Law of Northern Ireland
KDG		Law of Isle of Man and the Channel Islands
KDK		Law of Ireland (Eire)
		Law of Canada
KE		Federal law. Common and collective provincial law

Law		
KEA-KEY		Law of individual provinces and territories
KEO		e.g. Ontario
KEQ		Quebec
KEZ		Law of individual cities, A-Z
		Law of the United States
KF		Federal law. Common and collective state law
KFA-KFW		Law of individual states
KFA	0–599	e.g. Alabama
	1200–1799	Alaska
KFW	0–599	Washington
KFX		Law of individual cities, A-Z
KFZ		Law of individual territories

The Dewey decimal system identifies the main divisions by numbers rather than letters: for instance, 100 for Philosophy, 300 for Social Sciences, 800 for Literature, and 900 for Geography and History. Political Science, Public Administration, and Law are sub-classifications of Social Science.

Dewey Decimal Classification

Social Sciences
300 Social sciences
301   Sociology
302   Social interaction
303   Social processes
304   Relation of natural factors
305   Social stratification
306   Culture and institutions
307   Communities
308
309
310 Statistics
311
312   Statistics of populations

Social Sciences

313
314　General statistics of Europe
315　General statistics of Asia
316　General statistics of Africa
317　General statistics of North America
318　General statistics of South America
319　General statistics of other areas

320　Political science
321　Kinds of governments and states
322　Relation of state to social groups
323　Relation of state to its residents
324　The political process
325　International migration
326　Slavery & emancipation
327　International relations
328　Legislation
329

330　Economics
331　Labor economics
332　Financial economics
*333　Land economics
334　Cooperatives
335　Socialism & related systems
336　Public finance
337　International economics
338　Production
339　Macroeconomics & related topics

340　Law
341　International law
342　Constitutional & administrative law
343　Miscellaneous public law
344　Social law
345　Criminal law
346　Private law
347　Civil procedure & courts
348　Statutes, regulations, cases
349　Law of individual states & nations

Social Sciences

---

350 Public administration
351   Central governments
352   Local governments
353   U.S. federal & state governments
354   Other central governments
355   Military art & science
356   Foot forces & warfare
357   Mounted forces & warfare
358   Armored, technical, air, space forces
359   Sea (Naval) forces & warfare

360 Social problems & services
361   Social problems & welfare
362   Social welfare problems & services
363   Other social problems & services
364   Criminology
365   Penal institutions
366   Association
367   General clubs
368   Insurance
369   Miscellaneous kinds of associations

370 Education
371   Generalities of education
372   Elementary education
373   Secondary education
374   Adult education
375   Curriculums
376   Education of women
377   Schools & religion
378   Higher education
379   Education & the state

380 Commerce (Trade)
381   Internal commerce
382   International commerce
383   Postal communication
384   Other systems of communication
385   Railroad transportation
386   Inland waterway & ferry transportation

Social Sciences
387 Water, air, space transportation
388 Ground transportation
389 Metrology & standardization
390 Customs, etiquette, folklore
391 Costume & personal appearance
392 Customs of life cycle & domestic life
393 Death customs
394 General customs
395 Etiquette (Manners)
396
397
398 Folklore
399 Customs of war & diplomacy

Step 5: Read and Take Notes on Appropriate Books and Articles

Earlier in this chapter we explained the system of using index cards for recording your references as you discovered them (see Figure 7.1). When you are ready to begin reading those sources, you use the same cards to take notes. Information from each source (e.g., journal article, encyclopedia entry) is recorded on the bibliography card. Use the back of the card if you need more space. Occasionally, you'll need even more room; make a continuation card, headed by the author's last name and a shortened title. If you often find yourself using two or more cards for each source, though, chances are you are not digesting the material very well. You are probably copying long quotations that you will never use. Save time by making the condensation immediately after you have read the piece, while it is fresh in your understanding. Then write a summary of the major points.

Careful, responsible use of sources is the hallmark of the conscientious researcher. Inaccurate quotations and misleading summaries cause the reader to question the value of the entire piece of research. Whenever you use the words, ideas, data, or line of reasoning of another writer, you assume the responsibility of representing that author's work fairly and accurately and of crediting the source in the manner accepted by the discipline. See Chapter 8 for rules on documenting sources in political science.

The following passage, taken from an article on affirmative action, represents the source material that a researcher might want to use for a research report. Our treatment of summary, paraphrase, and quotation takes its examples from this passage:

> Comparable worth may indeed be an idea whose time has come. Where does it come from? When the plumber makes a house call and charges $40 an hour to fix a leak, the instinct of most people is to suspect that the plumber is overpaid — the beneficiary of some combination of scarce skills, powerful unions, and dumb luck. The instinct of comparable worth advocates is to see the plumber's wage as a standard of fairness, to conclude that the rest of us (meaning: women) are underpaid, and to identify discrimination as the source of that underpayment. But since overt discrimination on the basis of sex has been legally forbidden for twenty years, to make that charge stick nowadays requires a bit of subtlety.

Summary

The most efficient method of note-taking, summary is economical. A good summary of an eleven-page article might be only a hundred words or so. Just how you summarize depends on the source and your intended use of it. In one case, the entire article might be relevant to your needs; then you would write a comprehensive summary that followed the structure of the original closely, even including some of the evidence. In another situation, you might be more concerned with getting just the central idea of the article; two or three sentences could capture that for you. Another time you might find only one section of the article relevant to your needs, so you summarize only that section. In all cases, use your own words when summarizing the work of the author. Only two other rules apply to writing summaries: You must present the central idea of the original without distortion and you must credit the source both in your text with a citation and at the end of the paper in the list of works cited.

Paraphrase

Paraphrase is the running restatement of the information or ideas of another writer in your own words. Unlike a summary, which greatly condenses the information, the rewording of a paraphrase may be nearly as long as the original. It usually follows the same order of ideas as the original.

Original

> "The instinct of comparable worth advocates is to see the plumber's wage as a standard of fairness, to conclude that the rest of us (meaning: women) are underpaid, and to identify discrimination as the source of that underpayment" (Krauthammer, 1984, p. 16).

Paraphrase

> Proponents of comparable worth point to the plumber's high wages as indication that most other workers, especially women, are underpaid, and blame that situation on sexual discrimination.

Quotation

Unlike paraphrase and summary, quotation employs the exact words of the source. You must use great care to assure that the wording, spelling, punctuation, and data are precisely as they appear in the original. Although the use of quotation can be powerful, it is often overdone by those who fail to understand that readers are not necessarily impressed by frequent quotation and that overuse lessens its impact. Furthermore, quotation is uneconomical. A one-hundred-word quotation can be paraphrased in perhaps forty words or summarized in twenty. Include a quotation when the words and sentence structure of the original are significant or when the identity of the author is important to your case.

Quoted passages must be enclosed in quotation marks (" "). To delete material from within a quotation, use ellipsis periods (. . .) to mark the deletion: "The instinct of comparable worth advocates is . . . to conclude that the rest of us (meaning: women) are underpaid, and to identify discrimination as the source of that underpayment" (Krauthammer, 1984, p. 16). To add material for purposes of clarification, use brackets ([   ]) to enclose the added words: "The instinct of comparable worth advocates is to see the plumber's wage [$40 an hour] as a standard of fairness, to conclude that the rest of us (meaning: women) are underpaid, and to identify discrimination as the source of that underpayment" (Krauthammer, 1984, p. 16). As with paraphrase and summary, the writer must credit the sources of a quotation. See Chapter 8 for details.

Photocopying

No matter how proficient you become at taking notes, you will find that you have to photocopy some things — a table, a figure, a particularly pertinent article. By all means take them to the photocopy machine and make a copy. Copyright laws permit such copying, provided you note the source on your copy. You will need this information when citing the material in your paper. Copy what you must, but use some common sense. Some students will plug rolls of nickels into the copier rather than read anything in the library.

The Researcher's Sources

What are the primary sources on which researchers take notes in preparation for the writing of a political science paper? They are articles, books, government documents, legal publications, newspapers, and data bases.

A. Political Science Journals

One of the most common errors students make in compiling a list of works consulted is to restrict the list to books, and omit periodicals. Articles in scholarly journals provide up-to-date and specific information on topics that often cannot be found in books. You can strengthen your paper's bibliography considerably by including citations to scholarly articles. Each journal is refereed, meaning that the articles published in each issue have been reviewed favorably by recognized scholars in the appropriate subfield. This process assures you that the author has met the standards in the discipline for accuracy of data and soundness of conclusions based on that data. There are many political science journals, but the five that lead the discipline are:

American Political Science Review (1906--). Washington, D.C.: American Political Science Association.

Journal of Politics (1939--). Gainesville, Florida: Southern Political Science Association.

American Journal of Political Science (1957--). Austin: University of Texas Press.

Polity: The Journal of the Northeastern Political Science Association (1968--). Amherst: University of Massachusetts.

Western Political Quarterly (1948--). Salt Lake City: University of Utah.

Each of these journals covers all the subfields of political science. They are indexed/abstracted in *International Political Science Abstracts, United States Political Science Documents, Social Sciences Index, ABC Pol Sci, America: History and Life* and *Public Affairs Information Service.*

B. Book Reviews

The bulk of most students' reading lists consists of books. It is not enough to know how to find the appropriate books; you must also know how to evaluate them. Evaluation is necessary because books vary widely in quality. The best source of book reviews written by scholars is political science journals. A recently published book is often reviewed in several journals. You can locate the reviews of a particular book by consulting the book review section of the following indexes:

Social Sciences Index and *America: History and Life.*

A valuable periodical that reviews books useful in political science research within sixty days of their publication is:

Perspective: Monthly Review of New Books in Government, Politics and International Affairs (1972--). Washington, D. C.: Helen Dwight Reed Educational Foundation.

C. Government Publications

Government documents are rich sources of information often over-looked by student researchers. They include such diverse publications as the records of congressional debates and hearings, treaties, presidential messages, and studies commissioned by government agencies. Material is available on all political science subfields. State and local governments also produce useful documents. To track down government publications that will shed light on your topic you will need to consult an index. The best ones are:

Palic, V. M. (1975). *Government publications: A guide to bibliographic tools* (4th ed.). Washington, D.C.: Library of Congress.

Lists the publications of state and local governments, foreign governments, and international organizations, as well as those of the federal government.

U.S. Superintendent of Documents (1895--). *Monthly Catalog of United States Government Publications.* Washington, D.C.: Government Printing Office.

Catalogs all federal documents.

CIS/Index to Publications of the United States Congress (1970--). Washington, D.C.: James B. Adler.

Indexes and abstracts all congressional publications, including committee hearings and reports, some of the most valuable government documents for political science students.

U.S. Library of Congress (1910--). *Monthly Checklist of State Publications.* Washington, D.C.: Government Printing Office.

Indexes the 10,000 state publications issued each year.

UNDOC Current Index (1950--). New York: United Nations.

Catalogs UN documents relevant to your topic.

D. Legal Publications

Many political science courses are law related. Students with research assignments in these courses often turn to legal dictionaries, reports of judicial decisions, legislative codes, and legal periodicals. The standard source for the definitions of legal terms is:

Black, H. C. (1979). *Black's law dictionary.* Rev. 5th ed. St. Paul: West Publishing Co.

Reports of the decisions of the federal courts can be found in:

Federal Supplement (1933--). St. Paul: West Publishing Co.

Reports selected decisions of the U.S. District Courts.

Federal Reporter (1880--). St. Paul: West Publishing Co.

Reports decisions of the U.S. Courts of Appeals.

United States Reports (1754--). Washington, D.C.: Government Printing Office.

Reports all the decisions of the U.S. Supreme Court.

Students can locate decisions of state supreme courts by consulting:

A uniform system of citation (1981) (13th ed.). Cambridge, Mass.: The Harvard Law Review Association.

The most accessible source for federal laws is the:

United States Code (1983). Washington, D.C.: Government Printing Office.

Published every six years and supplemented annually. Contains all the federal laws in force at the time of publication.

The location of state laws can be identified by consulting *A uniform system of citation.*

Similar to political science journals, law reviews publish scholarly articles on legal topics, usually written by law professors. The two best sources of law review articles relevant to your topic are *ABC Pol Sci* and

Index to Legal Periodicals (1909--). New York: Wilson.

Published monthly.

A valuable use of this index is to trace the impact of an important court decision. For instance, in *INS v. Chadha* (1983), the Supreme Court invalidated the legislative veto, used by Congress in hundred of statutes to rein in the executive branch. If you wanted to know how significant the *Chadha* decision has proven to be, simply consult the case citation appendix of a recent issue of the *Index to Legal Periodicals*. Under *INS v. Chadha* you would find references to several law review articles that focus on the case, as shown in Figure 7.10.

```
Inmon; American Road Serv. Co. v., 394 So. 2d 361 (Ala.)
    34 Ala. L. Rev. 181-96 Wint '83
Inryco, Inc. v. Metropolitan Eng'r Co., 708 F.2d 1225
    45 U. Pitt. L. Rev. 695-717 Spr '84
INS v. Chadha, 103 S. Ct. 2764
    36 Ad. L. Rev. 239-76 Summ '84
    11 Brooklyn J. Int'l L. 79-101 Wint '85
    15 Cal. W. Int'l L.J. 201-302 Spr '85
    21 Cal. W.L. Rev. 174-94 Fall '84
    33 Cath. U.L. Rev. 811-62 Summ '84
    34 Cath. U.L. Rev. 485-524 Wint '85
    66 Chi. B. Rec. 98-100+ S/O '84
    33 Clev. St. L. Rev. 145-89 '84/'85
    69 Cornell L. Rev. 1244-66 Ag '84
    53 Geo. Wash. L. Rev. 168-90 Ja '85
    36 Hastings L.J. 1-92 S '84
    12 Hofstra L. Rev. 593-616 Spr '84
    11 J. Legis. 317-47 Summ '84
    49 Mo. L. Rev. 404-21 Spr '84
    11 Ohio N.U.L. Rev. 841-70 '84
    45 Ohio St. L.J. 983-1001 '84
    5 Pub. Land L. Rev. 55-67 Spr '84
    24 Santa Clara L. Rev. 697-741 Summ '84
    24 Santa Clara L. Rev. 243-69 Wint '84
    1983 Sup. Ct. Rev. 125-76 '83
    35 Syracuse L. Rev. 749-61 '84
    35 Syracuse L. Rev. 685-761 '84
    35 Syracuse L. Rev. 703-13 '84
    35 Syracuse L. Rev. 735-48 '84
    17 U. Mich. J.L. Ref. 743-70 Spr '84
    132 U. Pa. L. Rev. 1217-41 Je '84
    45 U. Pitt. L. Rev. 673-93 Spr '84
    18 U. Rich. L. Rev. 121-36 Fall '83
    59 Wash. L. Rev. 549-64 Jl '84
    94 Yale L.J. 1493-511 My '85
INS v. Delgado, 104 S. Ct. 1758
    70 A.B.A. J. 115-16 N '84
    18 Akron L. Rev. 339-50 Fall '84
    33 Clev. St. L. Rev. 323-38 '84/'85
```

Figure 7.10

E. General Periodicals

Political science journals and law reviews are not the only periodicals students will wish to utilize in their research. A number of publications addressed to general audiences are helpful sources for many topics. The two most useful types are news magazines (such as *Time, Newsweek,* and *U.S. News & World Report*) and magazines of political opinion (such as *New York Times Magazine, Commentary, Harper's, Atlantic Monthly, The New Republic,* and *National Review*). Most magazines of this type speak from a particular political point of view, generally either a liberal or conservative one. To identify the editorial slant of a particular periodical see:

> Katz, W. & Katz, L. S. (1982). *Magazines for libraries* (4th ed.). New York: Bowker.

Articles in these magazines are indexed in:

> *Reader's Guide to Periodical Literature* (1905--). New York: Wilson.

F. Newspapers and Press Digests

When conducting research on current issues, students find these newspapers especially good sources of information on national and international issues: *The New York Times, The Wall Street Journal,* and *The Washington Post.* Each of these papers is indexed:

> *The New York Times Index* (1913--). New York: The New York Times.

Provides abstracts of each article.

> *The Wall Street Journal Index* (1958--). New York: Dow Jones & Co.

Provides abstracts of each article.

> *Washington Post Index* (1972--). Worster, Ohio: Newspaper Indexing Center.

Presents headlines only, no abstracts.

Foreign newspapers are a significant source of information for students in international relations and comparative government courses. If your library does not subscribe to a particular foreign paper, or you do not read the language in which it is written, you will find the following press digests indispensable:

> *World Press Review* (1961--). New York: Atlas Information Services, Inc.

Appears monthly and contains excerpts and complete articles in English translation from foreign newspapers.

> The American Association for the Advancement of Slavic Studies (1929--). *Current Digest of the Soviet Press.* Columbus, Ohio: Ohio State University Press.

Published weekly, this source contains translations of all the significant articles from over sixty Soviet magazines and newspapers.

G. Sources of Quantitative Data

Political science students often consult handbooks, yearbooks, almanacs, and polls when they are seeking quantitative data. Because the information in books and articles is usually dated, students must consult handbooks and annuals for current information. Handbooks supply generally accepted facts. Yearbooks and almanacs, which are published annually, provide even more up-to-date information. General almanacs address a more popular audience than yearbooks and do not treat the data in as much depth. Public opinion poll results are useful in a variety of political science writing. Three useful handbooks are:

> *Book of the States* (1935--). Lexington, Kentucky: Council of State Government.

Published every two years. Provides factual and statistical information about the governments of each of the fifty states. A student writing a paper on the grand jury or the death penalty could find out which states employ them and which do not.

> U.S. Bureau of the Census (1879--). *County and City Data Book.* Washington, D.C.: Government Printing Office.

Published every four years. Contains statistics concerning the economy and population of all U.S. cities and counties. A student testing the hypothesis whether the crime rate is related to unemployment would consult this book to discover the necessary statistical information.

> Scammon, R. M. (Ed.). (1966--). *America votes: A handbook of contemporary American election statistics.* Washington, D.C.: Congressional Quarterly.

Biennial compilation of voting statistics covering all national elections since 1954. Breaks down the vote by states and counties.

Political science students find two yearbooks particularly useful:

> *Europa Yearbook* (1959--). London: Europa Publications.

Provides information for all countries, not just those in Europe, although its coverage of the latter is superb. Provides economic and demographic statistics as well as information on each nation's constitution and government.

> *Statistical Abstract of the United States* (1878--). Washington, D.C.: Government Printing Office.

Considered the most reliable source of statistics on American economy, society, and politics. The subject index is a convenient guide to specific statistical tables.

Because almanacs seek to cover broader subject areas than in handbooks, their coverage of any particular subject is less thorough. The almanac most frequently consulted by students of politics is:

> *World Almanac* (1868--). New York: Newspaper Enterprise Association.

Focuses upon the United States but presents information on all countries.

If you are writing a research report, you may wish to use a data base, which contains quantitative information. The database most frequently used by students shows the results of public opinion polls. Polls are helpful to students who wish to document public support for or opposition to a particular policy or who wish to test an empirical hypothesis. To find the Gallup Poll most relevant to your topic, see the following monthly publication:

Gallup Opinion Index (1965--). Princeton, N.J.: Gallup International.

$\begin{bmatrix} 8 \end{bmatrix}$ *Documentation Style Sheet*

> PREVIEW: *Documentation means giving proper credit for borrowed information. This chapter explains how to document your research in the widely accepted APA style.*
> *Citations*
> *References*

Almost everyone embarking on a project of research and writing finds the issue of documentation confusing. Should you use footnotes or in-text citations? A bibliography containing all the works consulted or a list of only those references cited? Which of many formats should you follow? Turabian, MLA (Modern Language Association), CBE (Council of Biological Editors), APA (American Psychological Association) — all have their advocates. Because of its wide acceptance in the social sciences, we have chosen to present the APA format as established in the *Publication Manual of the American Psychological Association* (third edition). Before you begin a course project, though, you should consult your professor on choice of style. If you are writing for publication, check the journals in the field. Each editor spells out manuscript requirements and other guidelines for contributors; look near the table of contents.

In the following pages you will find explanations and examples of the most common types of citations and references. Yet no brief treatment will likely answer all of your questions about manuscript preparation and documentation. If you don't find an answer to your question here, consult with your professor or with the APA manual, which is probably in your library's reference section.

For all practical purposes, footnotes or endnotes are hardly used anymore. Include a note only if you must add essential information that supplements, but cannot be integrated into, the text. Notes should be numbered consecutively throughout the paper.

Type raised arabic numerals like this to call attention to a note.[1] Type all notes on a separate sheet, headed Footnotes.

CITATIONS

When using the words, data, or ideas of another writer, you credit the source by means of a citation. This enables the reader to locate the source in the list of references at the end of your essay. APA citation style is fairly easy to learn and simple to use. The author's last name and the year of publication are inserted parenthetically in the text. Include the page number as well if you have used a paraphrase or summary of a passage or a direct quotation.

```
According to a recent study of voting records
(Hersh, 1985)
```

If the author's name and/or the date are mentioned in the text, they should be omitted from the parenthetical information.

```
A 1985 study of voting records (Hersh) shows

Hersh's study of voting records (1985) shows

In 1985 Hersh demonstrated
```

A Work by Two Authors

Cite both names each time the reference occurs.

```
A survey of court decisions found "little evidence
of stiffer sentencing and less of any effects of
the new pressure groups" (Howes & Ashton, 1981, p.
37).
```

[The page number refers to the location of the quotation.]

A Work by More Than Two and Fewer Than Six Authors

Cite all names in the first reference; after that, use only the surname of the first author followed by "et al."

```
(Costello, Jarvis, Koonze, & Sims, 1986) [first citation]

(Costello et al., 1986) [subsequent citations]
```

A Work by Six or More Authors

Cite the surname of the first author followed by "et al."

> This was disputed by Surtes et al. (1982)

A Work by an Institutional Author

Authorship of a work is sometimes attributed to a society, a government agency, or some other institution. In this case, the institution is cited as the author.

> (American Political Science Association, 1979)

Common abbreviations may be used or an abbreviation established in the first citation to be used subsequently, provided the meaning is clear.

> (UNESCO, 1977) [common abbreviation]
>
> (American Federation of Teachers [AFT], 1986) [first citation]
>
> (AFT, 1986) [subsequent citations]

A Work With No Author Given

When a book or article appears without an author's name, use the title instead. [Pamphlets, magazine and newspaper articles, and even books may lack a byline.]

> ("New bill aimed at lobbyists," 1985)

Entire Issue of a Journal

> ("Dispute Processing," 1980–81)

Two or More Works Within Parentheses

Works by the same author(s) are arranged in order of publication.

> (St. Cyr, 1977, 1983)

Works by different authors are arranged alphabetically by surnames.

> Several studies have reached the same conclusion (Larkin & Helmholz, 1979; Petkoff, 1966; Thomas, 1981).

Personal Communication [letters, interviews, phone conversations].

> Senator Henry Jackson (personal communication, October 12, 1977)

Personal communications are not included in the list of references because they cannot be consulted by the reader.

Government Documents

> (U.S. Internal Revenue Service, 1984)

Government Hearings

> (Sussman, 1984)

Court Cases

> (Munn v. Illinois, 1876)

Statutes

> (Federal Salary Act, 1967)

See *A Uniform System of Citation* (1981) for more details.

REFERENCES

The list of references at the end of an article or paper identifies the sources used, enabling the reader to locate those sources. This list includes every reference cited in the paper and no other. Although each part of a paper should be done with great care, compiling the list of references calls for exacting precision. A misspelled name, an incorrect page number, an omitted date — any of these will trouble the reader and call into question the accuracy of the research and the researcher.

The list of references begins on a separate page. The word References is centered at the top. The entries are listed alphabetically by the authors' last names or, in the case of institutional authorship, by the first significant word of the name. Use hanging indention: The first line of each entry begins at the left margin; subsequent lines are indented three spaces. Capitalize only the first word of the title and the subtitle of books and articles. Capitalize all important words in the names of journals and annuals. For journals, give the issue number in parentheses after the volume number only if each issue begins on page 1.

Rokeach, M. (1973). Beliefs, attitudes and values. San Francisco: Jossey-Bass.

References to Periodicals

Journal Article by One Author

Jackson, J. E. (1983). The systematic beliefs of the mass public: Estimating policy preferences with survey data. Journal of Politics, 45, 840–865.

Journal Article by Two Authors

Abramson, P. R., & Aldrich, J. H. (1982). The decline of electoral participation in America. American Political Science Review, 76, 502–521.

Journal Article by More Than Two Authors

Nie, N., Powell, B., & Prewitt, K. (1969). Social structure and political participation. American Political Science Review, 63, 361–378.

Journal Article in Press

Curtis, D. (in press). The courts and the congress. Journal of Legal Studies.

Magazine Article

Brodeur, P. (1985, June 10). Annals of law: The asbestos industry on trial I. The New Yorker, pp.
49–101.

Newspaper Article

Kaufman, M. (1985, August 4). Are things looser in
the eastern bloc? Yes and no. The New York Times,
p. 42.

Newspaper Article, No Author

Agency revises rules on asbestos to stress sealing
off of mineral. (1985, August 7). The Wall Street
Journal, p. 3.

Entire Issue of a Journal

Grossman, J., & Trubak, D. (Eds.). (1980–81). Dispute processing and civil litigation [Special is-
sue]. Law and Society Review, 15.

Monograph

M.I.T. System Dynamics Group. (1980). The outward
vs. inward paradigm and the management of social
systems. Conceptual Monograph No. 2 (D–2456), 1–
24.

Periodical Published Annually

Dawes, R. M. (1980). Social dilemmas. Annual Review
of Psychology, 31, 169–193.

Review of a Book

Larson, J. S. (1985). Review of Contemporary public
policy analysis. American Political Science Review, 79, 290.

References to Books

Book by One Author

> Truman, D. (1971). The governmental process (2d
> ed.). New York: Knopf.

Book by Two or More Authors

> Enelow, J. N., & Hinich, M. J. (1984). The spatial
> theory of voting: An introduction. New York: Cam-
> bridge University Press.

Book by an Institutional Author

> Small Business Administration. (1983). The state of
> small business. Washington: Government Printing
> Office.

Edited Book

> Schmidt, S., Scott, J., Lande, C., & Guasti, L.
> (Eds.). (1977). Friends, followers, and factions.
> Berkeley: University of California Press.

Chapter in a Book

> Brady, D. W. (1980). Congressional elections and
> clusters of policy changes in the U.S. House,
> 1886–1960. In B. A. Campbell & R. R. Trilling
> (Eds.), Realignments in American politics: Toward
> a theory (pp. XX–XXX). Austin: University of
> Texas Press.

Governmental Hearings

> Sussman, L. R. (1984). Testimony in U.S. withdrawal
> from UNESCO: Hearings before the Subcommittee on
> Human Rights and on International Operations of
> the Committee on Foreign Affairs, House of Repre-
> sentatives, April 25 and 26 and May 2, pp. 204–
> 229.

Reports

U.S. Internal Revenue Service. (1984). <u>1981 Statis-
tics of Income: Corporation Income Tax Returns</u>.
Washington, D.C.: U.S. Government Printing
Office.

Court Cases

<u>Munn v. Illinois</u>. (1876). 94 U.S. 113.

Statutes

Federal Salary Act of 1967, 2 U.S.C. 356 (1976).

References to Unpublished Sources

Unpublished Manuscript

Alt, J. E. (1981). <u>The politics of economic expectations.</u> Unpublished manuscript, Washington University, St. Louis.

Unpublished Paper Presented at a Meeting

Harris, P. (1980). <u>Problematic cases and the judicial search for authority</u>. Paper presented at the
annual meeting of the Law & Society Association,
Madison, WI.

[9] *A Concise Guide to Usage*

PREVIEW: *In this chapter we present nine rules of effective writing, chosen because they are so often violated by the unwary writer. Read through the chapter to familiarize yourself with the material, then refer to it again as you revise and proofread your work.*

Usage is the name given to matters of correctness or suitability of language — it's as simple as that. Most of us learn standard usage from parents, friends, teachers, newspapers and books, radio, and television. But we all have lapses and weak points that can be distracting to our readers. That is the reason for this section of the *Writer's Guide*. The rules explained below cover the most common questions of usage. Mastering them will not make you one of the world's great prose stylists, but it will help you to write more clearly, and without distracting your reader with usage errors.

RULE 1. SUBJECT AND VERB MUST AGREE IN NUMBER.

In English, nouns (and pronouns) and verbs are either singular or plural. If the subject noun (or pronoun) is singular, then the verb of the sentence must also be singular.

[singular subject] Ellen (She)   [singular verb] swims.
[plural subject] The girls (They)   [plural verb] swim.

So far, so good. But sentences like these aren't the ones that give writers problems. The difficulty surfaces when you write a sentence like this one:

The value placed on a free press by the two countries differ drastically.

Does that look all right to you? Let's see: The subject is *value,* singular; the verb is *differ,* plural. Subject and verb do not agree. This kind of error is common, especially in speaking, where it is easy to make. You hear the noun nearest to the verb, *countries,* and create a plural verb to match. Of course, *countries* is not the subject; *value* is. The correct sentence reads:

> The value placed on a free press by the two countries differs drastically.

A simple test for complicated sentences is to omit everything but subject and verb, then look and listen:

> The value . . . differs. . . .

Collective nouns name a group or collection: *herd, club, nation, team,* etc. They take a singular verb if unity is stressed or a plural verb if their plurality is emphasized: "The faculty *is* empowered to revise the curriculum" but "The faculty *are* divided on the issue of required courses."

RULE 2. A PRONOUN MUST AGREE IN NUMBER WITH ITS ANTECEDENT.

If the antecedent (the noun that the pronoun replaces) is singular, the pronoun must be singular. If the antecedent is plural, the pronoun must be plural:

> Some students [plural antecedent] fail to submit their [plural pronoun] papers on time.

This would seem an easy rule to follow, yet mistakes are common. One student's explanation of how to teach windsurfing contained this sentence: "Let the learner practice until they feel quite comfortable." Here the subject ("learner") is singular, but the pronoun ("they") is plural: "Let learners practice until they feel quite comfortable." This solution avoids the problem of gender introduced by the alternative: "Let the learner practice until he (she? he or she?) feels quite comfortable."

RULE 3. USE THE CORRECT FORM OF THE PRONOUN.

The common personal pronouns (I, me, he, him, she, her, it, we, us, you, they, them) seldom cause much difficulty. Many writers do have problems with the punctuation of two classes of possessive pronouns. Never use an apostrophe with these forms:

possessive forms (act as modifiers)

my	*my* pen
your	*your* books
his	*his* belt
her	*her* car
its	*its* clarity
our	*our* house
your	*your* camera
their	*their* papers

substantive forms (act as nouns)

mine	That pen is *mine*.
yours	Which books are *yours?*
his	The brown belt is *his*.
hers	The second car is *hers*.
its	Of the wines tested for clarity, *its* is best.
ours	The yellow house is *ours*.
yours	What kind of camera is *yours?*
theirs	The papers on the desk are *theirs*.

Note: it's is a contraction of *it is*.

RULE 4. DON'T SHIFT VERB TENSES UNNECESSARILY.

Traditionally, writers in some fields use only the past tense of verbs, treating all events and ideas as if they occurred in the past. Writers in other fields may sometimes use the historical present, treating past events as if they were happening now: "Shakespeare frequently alternates scenes of terror and tragedy with moments of comic relief." Use whichever tense best suits your needs. Just be consistent: Don't shift from past to present to past without a purpose.

RULE 5. PLACE MODIFIERS AS CLOSE AS POSSIBLE TO WORDS MODIFIED.

Writers-in-training are more apt to violate this rule with multi-word modifiers:

> Mangy and flea-bitten, I saw the dog sitting on my front steps.
>
> Our agency rents cars to salespeople of all sizes.
>
> Bouncing off parked cars, he spotted the driverless truck.

The meaning is clarified by placing the modifiers next to the words described:

> I saw the mangy and flea-bitten dog sitting on my front steps.
>
> Our agency rents cars of all sizes to salespeople.
>
> He spotted the driverless truck bouncing off parked cars.

RULE 6. WRITE COMPLETE SENTENCES.

A **sentence** is a group of words that contains a subject and a verb and expresses a complete thought. This is a sentence:

> My shoe is tight.

This is not a sentence:

> Because my shoe is tight.

Why not? What's the difference? Each group of words has a subject, *shoe*, and a verb, *is*. The only difference between the utterances is the addition of the word *because* to the second. The reason that "Because my shoe is tight" is not a sentence is that it doesn't express a complete thought; it cannot function as an independent unit.

Read it aloud, and you'll see what we mean. The listener (reader) is left dangling — because my shoe is tight *what?*[1]

Ironically, by adding a word, *because,* to the sentence, we've made it less than complete. This kind of word is called a **subordinator.** One kind of subordinator is the **relative pronoun:** *which, that, who, whom, what,* and *whose* are examples. The **subordinating conjunction** is a second kind. Common subordinating conjunctions are *because, after, when, although, as, before, if, unless, until, when,* and *where.* Adding these subordinators to a clause makes that clause dependent:

"Because my shoe is tight" is an example of one kind of sentence fragment. It doesn't express a complete thought, it cannot stand alone. It must be part of a complete sentence, like this:

> My foot hurts because my shoe is tight.

The sentence above has two **clauses.** Because the first clause, *my foot hurts,* expresses a complete thought and can stand alone, it is called **independent.** Because the second clause does not express a complete thought and cannot stand alone, it is called **dependent.**

A complete sentence, then, must contain an independent clause. It may contain additional elements as well.

complete sentence (independent clause):

> Stan stopped smoking recently.

complete sentence (two independent clauses and coordinating conjunction):

> Stan stopped smoking recently, and he feels healthier.

complete sentence (dependent clause and independent clause):

> Since Stan stopped smoking recently, he feels healthier.

---

[1]Speech and writing have different requirements. In the following conversation, "because my shoe is tight" may function perfectly well: "Why are you limping?" "Because my shoe is tight."

RULE 7. AVOID COMMA SPLICE AND RUN-ON.

When independent clauses are joined, you must separate them with a comma plus *and, but, or, for, nor,* or *yet*; or with a colon; or with a semicolon. Violations of this rule are the comma splice and the run-on sentence.

> **wrong** The fluorescent light over the desk in my office isn't working, it hasn't worked since the painters were here. (comma splice)
>
> **correct** The fluorescent light over the desk in my office isn't working, and it hasn't worked since the painters were here.
>
> **correct** The fluorescent light over the desk in my office isn't working; it hasn't worked since the painters were here.

Note: See Chapter 10 for use of the colon.

RULE 8. DISTINGUISH BETWEEN HOMOPHONES.

Homophones are words pronounced alike but different in spelling and meaning. Using any of them incorrectly marks your writing as less than meticulous. You should master these common ones:

their, there, they're

> *their* is a possessive pronoun:
>
> > on their own, their books
>
> *there* has three common uses:
>
> 1. as an adverb meaning *in, at,* or *to that place*:
>
> > She is going to build an addition there.
>
> 2. as a noun meaning *that place:*
>
> > We live near there.
>
> 3. as a function word to introduce a clause:
>
> > There are only two choices in the matter.

they're is a contraction of *they are:*

> They're my best friends.

to, too, two

to is a preposition meaning *toward, as far as, until, etc.*:

> The road to Jeffersonville is closed.
>
> The second shift is from three to eleven.

With a verb, it is a sign of the infinitive:

> The plant manager likes to play squash.

too is an adverb meaning *also, more than enough*:

> The report was late too.
>
> Too many cooks spoil the broth.

two is the number between one and three, used as an adjective or a pronoun:

> "Two hamburgers, please."
>
> Only two survived.

than, then

than is a conjunction used in comparisons:

> She is taller than her brother.

then may be an adverb, adjective, or noun related to time:

> I'm going to the meeting too. I'll see you then.
>
> Since then he hasn't smiled.

RULE 9. AVOID SEXUALLY-BIASED LANGUAGE.

In recent years we have become much more aware of the ways language shapes our thinking. Most people realize that referring to Italians as "wops," for instance, not only demeans them but also makes it difficult for us to perceive Italians as anything but stereotypes.

I don't believe you're likely to practice racial or national stereotyping in your writing. But you and I along with millions of other

Americans do practice another kind of linguistic bias nearly every time we write. I'm talking about sexual bias. Let me show you what I mean:

> Pioneers moved West, taking their wives and children with them.

What's wrong with that sentence? It's the assumption that the pioneers, the builders of our nation, were all males and that women (and children) went along for the ride. That is simply not true. It is this kind of bias, perhaps unconscious, perhaps unintentional, that you need to watch for in your writing.

To be honest, avoiding sexist language isn't always easy. Because the English language lacks a singular pronoun that means *he or she,* the writer constantly has to deal with gender choices like these:

> When the shopper wishes to cash a check, she (he?)...

> Each student should write his (or her?) name at the top.

As a writer, you do have options:

1. Alternate female and male pronouns.

    A sprinter warms up by stretching her muscles. A pianist runs over scales and chords to limber his fingers.

2. Rewrite to use the plural.

    Sprinters warm up by stretching their muscles. Pianists run over scales and chords to limber their fingers.

3. Rewrite to avoid gender pronouns.

    A sprinter warms up by stretching. A pianist runs over scales and chords.

A Final Word

It is impossible in these few pages to anticipate all the questions you might have as you write your papers. Every writer should have a copy of a handbook of usage. Buy one and refer to it as you revise your papers. A few minutes spent in this way can make all the difference in the impact of your paper.

[10] *Make Punctuation Work for You*

> PREVIEW: *Correctly used, punctuation aids the reader's understanding of your writing. Incorrectly used, punctuation can confuse or misinform. This chapter focuses on the most common uses of each mark of punctuation. Read through the chapter to familiarize yourself with the material, then refer to it again as you revise and proofread your work.*

We use punctuation marks to clarify the meaning of our writing. Some usages are purely conventional — the colon (:) after "Dear Sir" in a business letter, for instance. Others have been established to make meaning clear. Your primary goal in punctuating should always be clarity of expression. Although common sense will often help you select the correct usage, there is no substitute for knowing a few basic rules.

Comma ,

The comma is the most frequently used, and abused, mark of punctuation. Relatively weak as a separator, it is less emphatic than the colon, semicolon, or dash. It indicates the briefest of pauses. Although there are dozens of uses of the comma, we'll look at only the most common.

To separate items in a series:

> The standard personal computer consists of memory, video display, keyboard, disc drive, and printer.

Note: a comma is used before the *and*.

To set off interrupters:

> The party's candidate fot governor, Marie Marshall, offered her plan to reduce the deficit. (appositive)

The flight from Chicago, on the other hand, arrived on time. (parenthetical expression)

Note: Interrupters are enclosed by a *pair* of commas.

To set off a long introductory phrase or clause:

In the deep snows at the top of the mountain, they hid a cache of supplies.

If you want to learn to ski the right way, you should take lessons.

To separate independent clauses joined by and, but, or, nor, for, yet:

Matt was interested in the job, but he didn't want to move away from his family.

The purchasing department ordered new furniture, and the office manager had the rooms painted.

To introduce a short quotation:

The librarian told them, "If you have a question, ask someone."

Semicolon ;

The semicolon provides more separation than the comma, less than the period. Its most common use is to separate independent clauses not joined by *and, but, or, nor, for, yet,* when you wish to show close relationship between those clauses. Otherwise, use a period.

The dean wanted a new curriculum; the faculty did not.

My mother was understanding the first time; she was upset the second time; the third time she was furious.

To Review: To show the degree of relationship between independent clauses, you have three options: semicolon, period, and comma with coordinating conjunction (*and, but, or, nor, for, yet*).

The legislature has been meeting since January; they have not passed a single bill.

The legislature has been meeting since January. They have not passed a single bill.

The legislature has been meeting since January, yet they have not passed a single bill.

Colon   :

The colon is used primarily to introduce a word, phrase, or clause that fulfills or explains an idea in the first part of the sentence. It is also used after the salutation of a business letter, to introduce a list, and to separate the title and subtitle of a book. Because it is a strong mark of punctuation, use it only as directed.

To introduce or fulfill:

In that respect, Canada is like the United States: Both have large numbers of non-English speakers.

On his deathbed the old miser made only one request: that his gold be buried with him.

To introduce a list:

The demographic study focused on three factors: population, income, and age.

Note: Do not use a colon directly after a verb.

wrong	On her trip to France she visited: Paris, Chartres, and Mont St. Michel.
correct	On her trip to France she visited Paris, Chartres, and Mont St. Michel.

After the salutation of a business letter:

Dear Mrs. Irving:

To separate the title and the subtitle of a book:

The Golden Bough: *A Study in Magic and Religion*

Apostrophe   '

The apostrophe has three distinct uses: to mark the omission of one or more letters or numerals, to mark the possessive case, and to mark certain plurals.

173

To mark the omission of a letter or letters:

wouldn't	(would not)
can't	(cannot)
you'll	(you will)
I'm	(I am)
it's	(it is)
they're	(they are)

To mark the omission of one or more numerals:

a '57 Chevy	a 1957 Chevy
the summer of '42	the summer of 1942

To form the possessive of a singular or plural noun not ending in s:

girl	girl's
laboratory	laboratory's
men	men's
children	children's

To form the possessive of a plural noun ending in s:

girls	girls'
books	books'
laboratories	laboratories'

To form the possessive of a singular noun of one syllable ending in s *or* s *sound:*

William James	William James's philosophy
Brahms	Brahms's First Symphony

To form the possessive of a singular noun of more than one syllable ending in s *or* s *sound:*

Socrates	Socrates' school

Note: Do not use an apostrophe with possessive pronouns: *his, hers, yours, ours, theirs, whose, its* (*it's* means *it is*).

Parentheses ( )

Parentheses are used to enclose explanatory material within a sentence when such material is incidental to the main thought. Commas may also be used for this purpose; they are less formal and indicate a closer relationship to the main sentence than parentheses. Some writers use parentheses for the same purpose.

> Senator Arndt (who just happens to be my brother-in-law) wrote the new farm credit bill.

> Of his many novels (he wrote more than thirty), *Stairway to Darkness* was his favorite.

Note: Parentheses are sometimes used in other ways in footnotes. See the section on documentation.

Brackets [ ]

Brackets are marks of punctuation with limited but specific uses, especially in academic writing. Often when you excerpt part of a longer quotation, the meaning is not entirely clear. You may add clarification in brackets.

> "The President [Truman] was determined that war policy be made by civilians, not generals."

> "Freud's division of the psyche [id, ego, superego] has been disputed by many in recent years."

When you wish to acknowledge without changing an error in the quoted material, enclose the Latin word *sic* (thus) in brackets:

> "The carriage careened wildly through muddy ruts until it broke an axel [**sic**]."

Note: Many typewriters do not have brackets. You can ink them in by hand. Do not use parentheses instead of brackets.

Ellipsis . . .

The omission (ellipsis) of part of a quoted passage is indicated by ellipsis marks: three spaced periods. Use these marks when you are quoting a long passage but wish to omit material.

"These matriarchal tribes . . . often fight small wars to extend their territory."

When you delete the end of a sentence, use four periods:

"Four score and seven years ago our fathers brought forth on this continent, a new nation. . . . Now we are engaged in a great civil war, testing whether that nation, or any nation so conceived and so dedicated, can long endure."

Dash —

The dash is probably the most overused mark of punctuation. Because it is so emphatic, its misuse stands out glaringly and is viewed as the sign of an overemotional style. Employ the dash only as described below.

To show an abrupt break in thought:

I explained all that to you yesterday when — oh, but that wasn't you.

To introduce a word or words for emphasis:

You have only one choice — do it!

To separate a final summarizing clause from the preceding idea:

Food, clothing, shelter, and fuel — these are all that Thoreau claimed are needed to sustain life.

Note: To type a dash, use two hyphens (--). Do not leave a space before or after the hyphens.

Quotation Marks " "

Quotation marks enclose the precise words spoken or written by someone other than the writer. Do not use them to identify indirect quotations or summaries.

To enclose direct quotations:

In his book, Bronsky asserts, "Mussolini's leadership was not entirely bad for Italy."

Franklin Delano Roosevelt's powerful words, "The only thing we have to fear is fear itself," were spoken in the depths of national depression.

Note: When the quoted passage is embedded in a sentence, it is preceded by a comma (and followed by one if the sentence continues beyond the quotation).

Exception: Long quotations (more than four typed lines) are indented ten spaces and double spaced. Quotation marks are not used. See section on documentation.

A quotation within a quotation uses single marks within double marks:

In her inaugural speech Governor Harris urged her listeners to "Remember President Kennedy's message 'Ask not what your country can do for you — ask what you can do for your country.'"

Note: Periods and commas are placed inside the quotation marks. Semicolons and colons are placed outside. Question marks, exclamation points, and dashes are placed outside the quotation marks unless they are part of the original quotation.

To mark the titles of short stories, poems, essays, articles, chapters of books, songs, symphonies, and plays in collections:

Hemingway's story "The Snows of Kilimanjaro"

Shelley's poem "To a Skylark"

Note: Titles of books, full-length plays, magazines, and newspapers are *italicized* or *underlined,* not placed in quotation marks.

References

APA. 1983. Publication Manual of the American Psychological Association. 3rd ed. Washington, D.C.: American Psychological Association.

Conway, M. M. & Feigert, F. B. (1972). *Political Analysis: An Introduction*. Boston: Allyn & Bacon.

Holland, K. (1983). Policy analysis of efforts to contain white-collar crime. In Nagel, S., Fairchild, E. & Champagne, A. (Eds.). *The Political Science of Criminal Justice*. Springfield, IL: Charles C. Thomas, 263–275.

Kipnis, K. (1976). Criminal justice and the negotiated plea. *Ethics, 86.*

Krauthammer, C. (1984, July 30). From bad to worth. *The New Republic*, 16–18.

Kremer, A. J. (1985, October 2). Letter. *The New York Times,* p. A. 26.

Lewis-Beck, M. S., & Alford, J. R. (1980). Can government regulate safety? The coal mine example. *American Political Science Review, 74, 745.*

McEwen, C. A., & Maiman, R. J. (1982). Arbitration and mediation as alternatives to court. *Policy Studies Journal, 10,* 712–713.

Nagel, S. (1985). Part/whole percentaging as a useful method in policy/program evaluation. *Evaluation and Program Planning, 8,* 107–120.

Orwin, C. (1984). The just and the advantageous in Thucydides: The case of the Mytilenaian debate. *American Political Science Review, 78,* 485.

Shively, W. P. (1974). *The Craft of Political Research: A Primer.* Englewood Cliffs, NJ: Prentice-Hall.

Wolfe, C. (1985). Book review. *American Political Science Review, 79,* 196–197.

Index